PUFFIN BOOKS

THE INCREDIBLE HISTORY OF THE INDIAN OCEAN

Sanjeev Sanyal is a prolific writer who writes for adults and children. He has also authored *The Incredible History of India's Geography* for a younger audience. Sanjeev Sanyal is the principal economic advisor to the Government of India and an internationally acclaimed economist and urban theorist. He writes on topics ranging from economics to history and is the author of the bestselling books *Land of the Seven Rivers* and *The Indian Renaissance*. In 2014, he was given the inaugural International Indian Achievers Award for contributions to literature. He has been a fellow of the Royal Geographical Society, London, visiting scholar at Oxford University, adjunct fellow at Institute of Policy Studies, Singapore and a senior fellow of the World Wide Fund for Nature. Sanjeev attended Shri Ram College of Commerce, Delhi and St John's College, Oxford, where he was a Rhodes Scholar. He lives in Delhi.

THE INCREDIBLE HISTORY HISTORY OF THE INDIAN OCEAN

An adaptation of *The Ocean of Churn* for young readers

SANJEEV SANYAL

Illustrations by Nikhil Gulati

PUFFIN BOOKS
An imprint of Penguin Random House

PUFFIN BOOKS

USA | Canada | UK | Ireland | Australia
New Zealand | India | South Africa | China

Puffin Books is part of the Penguin Random House group of companies
whose addresses can be found at global.penguinrandomhouse.com

Published by Penguin Random House India Pvt. Ltd.
4th Floor, Capital Tower 1, MG Road,
Gurugram 122 002, Haryana, India

First published in Puffin Books by Penguin Random House India 2020

Copyright © Sanjeev Sanyal 2020
Illustrations copyright © Jit Chowdhury 2016 and Nikhil Gulati 2020

Adapted from *The Ocean of Churn* by Ashwitha Jayakumar

Illustration of 'Stitched Ships' on page 93 reproduced
by permission from Nick Burningham

10 9 8 7

The views and opinions expressed in this book are the author's own and the facts
are as reported by him/her which have been verified to the extent possible, and the
publishers are not in any way liable for the same.

ISBN 9780143446019

Typeset in Adobe Caslon Pro by Manipal Technologies Limited, Manipal
Printed at Replika Press Pvt. Ltd, India

www.penguin.co.in

 *To Vedant, Veer and Dev—that they may one day explore the Indian Ocean*

CONTENTS

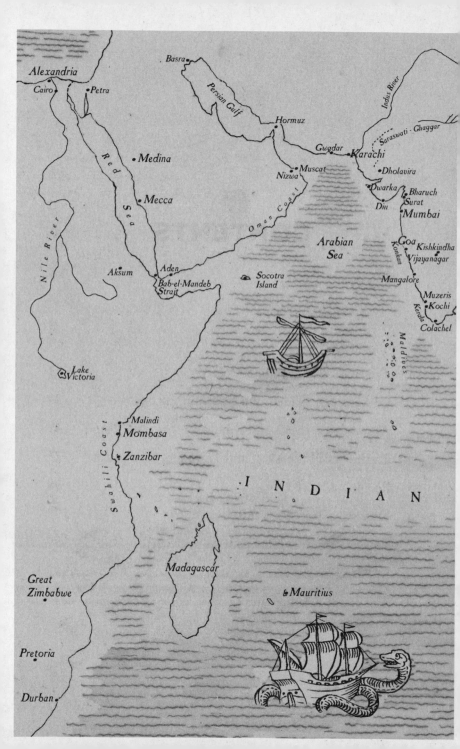

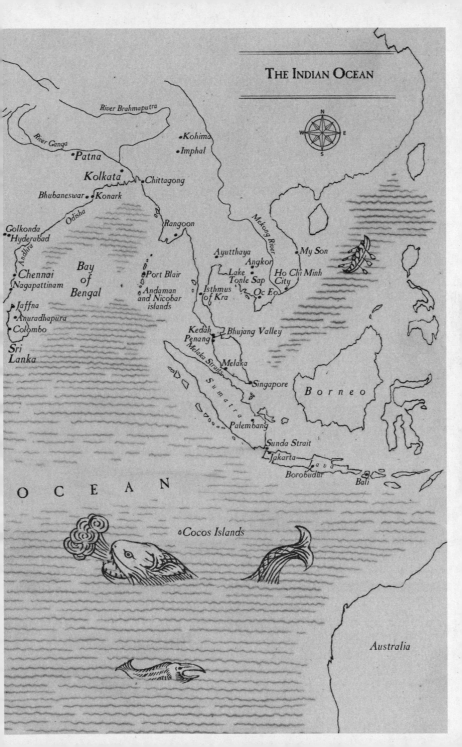

AUTHOR'S NOTE

This is my second attempt at adapting one of my books for a younger reader. My first attempt—*The Incredible History of India's Geography*—was an adaptation of *Land of the Seven Rivers*. I must admit I had not expected it to gain much of a following, but it seems to have developed a life independent of the original. At the time of writing, the book had already run through twenty-six editions. So I readily agreed when Sohini Mitra at Puffin suggested that I attempt an adaptation of *The Ocean of Churn*. After all, many of my younger readers live in the coastal cities and states that I describe in the book.

The problem was that, by this time, I was swamped with official work. So it fell upon Ashwitha Jayakumar to do the slog overs. It may not have been easy to deal with a distracted author and I thank both of them for their patience.

Nikhil Gulati put in a lot of effort with the illustrations. He obviously read the book very carefully and did a lot of research on his own. I would also like to thank Shalini Agrawal (copy editor) and Akangksha Sarmah (designer) who gave the book its final shape. As they say, publishing a book is a team sport.

CHAPTER 1

THE BIRTH OF THE INDIAN OCEAN

Going Back to the Beginning

On the morning of 26 December 2004, a powerful earthquake rocked the floor of the Indian Ocean near the island nation of Indonesia. What followed was a massive tsunami—a series of huge waves up to 100 feet high—that crashed on to the shores of countries bordering the Indian Ocean. From Bali in South East Asia all the way to the coast of East Africa, the tsunami brought an unprecedented level of destruction, leaving homes and buildings destroyed and washing away hundreds of thousands of people. The similarity of the devastation experienced by places so far away from each other was a reminder that diverse nations and peoples are connected by one body of water: the vast Indian Ocean.

Rescue parties sent out after the tsunami found that some groups of people were not as badly affected by the tsunami as nearly everyone else. Tribes such as the Onge and Jarawa, who inhabit the Andaman and Nicobar Islands, suffered almost no casualties despite being very close to the epicentre of the earthquake. Their ancestors, who first arrived on the islands over 30,000 years ago, had possibly experienced tsunamis, and their knowledge was preserved in the stories that the tribespeople told. Thus, they knew to move to higher ground when they felt the ground shake beneath their feet. In contrast, members of the Nicobarese tribes, whose ancestors settled there less than 600 years ago, didn't have a tradition of such stories and they suffered heavy casualties. Clearly, early settlers in the lands bordering the Indian Ocean had arrived at a time when it was not uncommon for enormous ocean waves to appear after the earth shook.

Tsunamis and Japan

The word 'tsunami' is a Japanese word. The country of Japan has experienced over 190 tsunamis in its recorded history, which is probably why they made up a special name for them. Tsunamis are most often caused by underwater earthquakes, although they can also be caused by underwater volcanic eruptions, landslides and even asteroids impacting the ocean.

But when did human beings first come to live here? What connections did they have to each other, and what do they still have in common? To answer these questions, we have to go back in time to the beginnings of the Indian Ocean.

How the Indian Ocean Was Made

Until about 100 years ago, people believed that the oceans and continents were fixed in place. In 1912, a geologist named Alfred Wegener came up with a theory in a book called *The Origin of Continents and Oceans*. Wegener argued that the seven continents that exist today had all been part of one giant land mass, a supercontinent named Pangaea. This supercontinent had begun to break up into pieces, with the pieces then gradually drifting apart from each other and into the positions they occupy today.

Wegener was not the first to come up with an idea like this. Since the sixteenth century, cartographers and geologists had been puzzled by the fact that the continents seemed shaped to fit together, like the pieces of a jigsaw puzzle: could they have once been joined together?

We now know that Wegener was on the right track. Various land masses did come together to form a massive supercontinent about 270 million years ago. Take a look at the map of Pangaea and you'll see that India, Australia, Madagascar, Antarctica and Africa were all stuck to each other—and that the Indian Ocean didn't even exist yet. About 175 million years ago, Pangaea began to break apart. It first broke into two large pieces called Laurasia and Gondwana. The land masses that we know today as North America, Europe and Asia were part of Laurasia, while Gondwana was made up of South America, Africa, Australia, India and Antarctica. Eventually, Laurasia and Gondwana broke up into even smaller pieces. India and Madagascar probably broke away from Africa about 160 million years ago and broke away from Antarctica and Australia about 130 million years ago. About 90 million years ago, India broke away from Madagascar and began drifting north. Between 85 and 45 million years ago, Australia and Antarctica separated, and the Australian plate moved north to fuse with the Indian plate, creating the Indo-Australian plate.

As it drifted north, the Indo-Australian plate collided with something in its way: the Eurasian plate. The force of the collision pushed the land upwards, creating the Himalayas. The land that was pushed upwards to create the Himalayas was once under the gigantic Tethys Sea, which encircled Pangaea. In fact, the fossils of sea creatures that were discovered on the mountains provided proof of plate tectonics, which is the idea that the Earth's

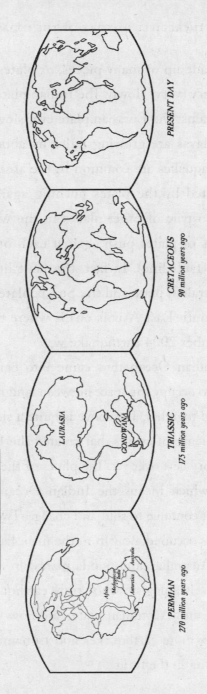

THE BREAK-UP OF PANGAEA

PERMIAN
270 million years ago

Africa
Madagascar
India
Antarctica
Australia

TRIASSIC
175 million years ago

LAURASIA

GONDWANA

CRETACEOUS
90 million years ago

PRESENT DAY

crust is made up of many pieces, or plates, that continue to move very (very) slowly. The Indian plate has continued to push against the Eurasian plate ever since, which is why the Himalayas are growing taller by about 5 mm every year. Earthquakes are common in the area because of the force exerted by the plates pushing against each other. This is also true of other places in the world where the boundaries of plates push against each other (geologists call this a fault line). In fact, the fault line between the Indo-Australian plate and the Sunda plate (the plate that most of South East Asia is on) is where the epicentre of the December 2004 earthquake was.

The Indian Ocean thus came into being when water rushed in to occupy the space between land masses that were once joined together. The above is quite a simplified version of the sequence of events that created the Indian Ocean—and the story isn't over yet. The plates of the Earth continue to move, which means the Indian Ocean and the lands bordering it continue to shift and change. Two more undersea earthquakes occurred away from the main fault line (between the Indo-Australian and Sunda plates) in April 2012. This has made seismologists who study earthquakes think that the Indian and Australian plates are now separating. That could bring more earthquakes and tsunamis to the Indian Ocean region in the future.

There are other things that are changing in the Indian Ocean too. The coastlines that we are familiar with didn't always look the way they do now. The sea level has changed over the years due to the warming and cooling of our planet. Since the last Ice Age, which occurred 18–20,000 years ago, the sea level has risen by 120 metres as the ice sheets have melted. This melting and the subsequent flooding of the coastlines have had a major impact on the history of our early ancestors, as we will see. The shifting of sand and silt by rivers and, of course, human activity, have also had an impact on the Indian Ocean landscape.

A Species on the Move

All of the movements described above took place a long, long time before any humans were around to observe them. We know about them now because of the hard work of geologists and scientists. Modern humans, *Homo sapiens* or 'wise man'—the species we all belong to—appeared between 2,00,000 and 3,00,000 years ago. At the time, this was not the only human species on the planet. The Neanderthals inhabited Europe and the Middle East, while their close cousins, the Denisovans roamed across Asia. There was even a small isolated group of dwarf humans, *Homo floresiensis*, who lived on the island of Flores, Indonesia until perhaps as recently as 12,000 years ago.

None of these other human species have survived, and they have not existed for a very long time.

Homo sapiens first appeared in the East African Rift Valley, a region that lies in modern-day Kenya and Malawi. Sometime after they first appeared in the area, at least one group decided to leave their original habitat to seek new lands to the north—theirs would have been the first human eyes to look out upon the Indian Ocean. Archaeological evidence tells us that this group travelled all the way to the Levant (the region immediately to the east of the Mediterranean, where Israel and Lebanon are today) about 1,20,000 years ago. This initial foray into the wider world was a failure, and these early explorers either died out or went back home.

Where did the Neanderthals go?

We do not know exactly why they died out about 24,000 years ago. Changes in climate may have played a role, but the arrival of *Homo sapiens* may also have had an impact. Perhaps they lost their best hunting grounds to *Homo sapiens* or fell prey to new diseases.

Interestingly, it was discovered some time ago that 1–4 per cent of the DNA of all non-Africans is derived from Neanderthals. There seems to have been some amount of mixing between the Neanderthals and *Homo sapiens*. This means that the Neanderthals did not entirely die out, as their genes live on within some of us.

About 65–70,000 years ago, it appears that a small group of *Homo sapiens* decided to venture out of their African homeland once more. The terrain these humans saw on their journey would have looked very different from what it looks like today. The climate of Earth was a lot cooler, sea levels were lower and shorelines were 50–100 kilometres further out than today's shorelines. It would have thus been easier for them to cross over from Djibouti in Africa to Yemen on the Arabian Peninsula.

This group of people who migrated out of Africa are said to be the genetic ancestors of all non-Africans on the planet. They made their way northwards through the Arabian Peninsula and eventually arrived at a lush green area near the Persian Gulf (near modern-day Saudi Arabia and Iran). They prospered here, and their numbers soon increased. They began to go further afield, all the way across the Makran coast (in modern-day Iran and Pakistan) into the Indian subcontinent. Although this area is a desert today, it was grassland that probably made for a good migration route 60,000 years ago. The coastline was also much further out, and what is now the Saurashtra peninsula of Gujarat was not a peninsula at all, but a continuous coastline.

The next big exploratory push seems to have occurred 50–55,000 years ago, when a small, adventurous group seems to have left the Persian Gulf-Indian subcontinent region and headed eastwards. They probably walked all the way along the Indian coast to what is now South East Asia. Since sea levels back then were a lot lower than they are today, the many islands in the area would have been connected to the mainland at that time. This would have helped the group travel more quickly and easily. The modern-day inhabitants of Fiji, Papua New Guinea and parts of Indonesia, called Melanesians, are descended from this group.

About 45,000 years ago, some of these ancient Melanesians went across to Australia. Even though sea levels were lower, this group of explorers still had a considerable journey to make, because Australia lay across a large body of water. They would have needed to know how to build rafts. These humans were the first to ever set foot on the continent, and their arrival would change the landscape forever. The animals and plants of Australia were (and are) unique and different because they developed in isolation from all other ecosystems in the region. Ancient Australia was home to some magnificent creatures, including 200-kilogram, two-metre-tall kangaroos, giant koalas and flightless birds that were twice the size of the modern ostrich. However, within a few thousand years of human beings arriving in Australia, all of these gigantic creatures died out, possibly owing to being hunted, landscape clearing and an increase in the number of certain kinds of plants.

We know almost nothing about the early human explorers who made the journeys described above—not their names, how they related to each other or how they saw the world. But they have left behind two very important things for us to remember them by.

The first is art. Cave paintings and handprints of both adults and children were discovered in the 1950s in Sulawesi, Indonesia. They were originally thought to be only 10,000 years old, but they have recently been dated to almost 40,000 years ago—among the oldest in the world. It is almost as if these ancient humans, both adults and children, are reaching out to us through the mists of time.

The second thing these ancient humans left us with is something smaller, an invisible part of all of us: our genes.

Ancient Migrations

As we have seen above, some groups chose to remain where they were, while others travelled further and further away from their point of origin. About 40,000 years ago, another group passed through India on their way to South East Asia, with some choosing to remain in India and some going ahead to populate the lands we know as Laos, Cambodia, Vietnam and southern China.

A recent study suggests that most people who live in this region today, including the Chinese, Japanese, Thai, Malay, Burmese, Filipino, as well as the inhabitants of the Polynesian islands and even some eastern Indian tribes, are all descended from this group. Some groups from the Persian Gulf region headed to Europe, some braved the freezing cold of Siberia and some even returned to Africa.

What is a gene?

Has anyone ever told you that you have your mother's eyes or your father's smile? Or perhaps you've noticed in family photos that you and your parents and siblings all share certain similarities. These similarities are all caused by genes. Genes are part of the long chains of DNA (Deoxyribonucleic acid) that contain the 'instruction manual' according to which our bodies are built. All living things have DNA, and all living organisms get their genes from their parents, who got it from their parents and so on. Over time, certain changes or mutations in genes occur in response to the environment or other factors. This is how evolution occurred.

One group, it is thought, headed towards southern India about 30–35,000 years ago and settled there. People who study genetics believe that this group contributed their genes to one of the two main genetic mixes all Indians are descended from, Ancestral South Indians (ASI) and Ancestral North Indians (ANI). Another group travelled all the way to the Andaman and Nicobar Islands, and were the ancestors of one of the tribes we heard about earlier, the Onge. Meanwhile, with all the coming and going of different groups, the genetic make-up of the population in the Persian Gulf-northern India region changed quite a lot over time. Geneticists believe that the second genetic mix modern-day Indians are descended from originated here.

ANCIENT MIGRATIONS
Routes taken by early explorers out of Africa

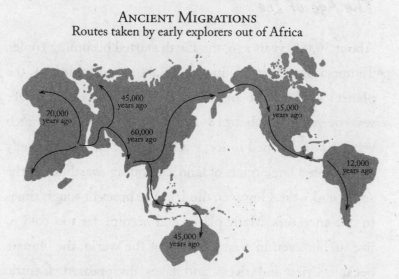

This, in a nutshell, is how different groups of human beings came to live in the lands bordering the Indian Ocean at various times in the distant past. There were probably many more groups of people who failed, turned back or died out. What's more, the story isn't complete yet. Genetic and archaeological evidence continues to flow in and fill in the gaps in this story. In the past, people have sometimes used genetics to 'prove' that one race of people is better or stronger than the others, but this isn't meaningful because a lot of different things determined which groups of people (and their genes) survived. Sometimes, it was just sheer luck!

The Age of Ice

About 30,000 years ago, the Earth started becoming cooler. Temperatures kept falling until about one-third of the planet's land surface and about half of the oceanic surface was covered in ice, about 18–20,000 years ago. With so much water having turned to ice, sea levels dropped dramatically and exposed large tracts of land, extending coastlines in the south and west. However, the Ice Age brought tough times to our ancestors. Many places had become far too cold to live in, but even in warmer parts of the world, the climate became drier and rivers and lakes disappeared. Central Asia became a cold, dry desert that couldn't support many animals or humans. The Himalayas were covered in glaciers and the north-western areas of India might have been temperate grasslands. In Africa, the Sahara and Kalahari deserts expanded, while the great Lake Victoria almost dried up.

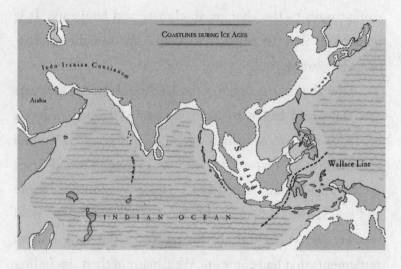

COASTLINES DURING ICE AGES

Indo-Iranian Continuum

Arabia

Sundaland

Wallace Line

INDIAN OCEAN

These changes forced different groups of humans to abandon their old hunting grounds and move closer to the remaining sources of water. For example, the Sahara grasslands had supported a large population, but the expansion of the desert forced people (and animals) to move closer to the banks of the Nile. Even the mighty Nile was not as broad as it had been and is today, but was a much shorter and narrower series of channels. Surrounded by a desert, the groups of people who settled near the river began to stay in this 'oasis' of sorts, which was about 800 kilometres in length and ran from modern-day Sudan to Cairo. The local population grew, and there is evidence that more and more people from the surrounding regions also made their way to this 'oasis'. People in other parts of the world presumably reacted in similar ways to the changes in climate and landscape. It is quite likely that the Indian Ocean rim also saw the creation of such communities.

After the coldest point of the Ice Age about 18,000 years ago, the world began to warm up again. Rising sea levels began to reshape coastlines again, while increased rainfall and melting ice revived the lakes and rivers that had dried up. By 12,500 years ago, Lake Victoria was full once more and the Sahara had reverted to being a grassland that could support life. What did all this mean for the early human settlements that had come up? Well, many of them, including the inhabitants of the Nile oasis, went back to being hunter-gatherers! The Indian Ocean rim also underwent a similar shift. Warmer weather, melting ice and increased rainfall had their impact on the landscape, and previously dry areas became much wetter and more habitable. A rise in sea levels meant that the Persian Gulf area became flooded and the coastline changed. The monsoons became stronger. This change in climate and landscape led to a great deal of human migration into areas that had previously been inhabitable.

From Hunters to Farmers

All of the groups of people we have been talking about so far were mainly hunter-gatherers. That meant they lived off whatever they could hunt or forage for. This also meant that they needed to move from place to place once they had used up all the food or water available in one region. But, we are told, at some point during the Neolithic period human beings discovered that they could grow the food they needed. This led to people exchanging a hunting-and-gathering lifestyle for one that involved building farms and villages and remaining settled in one area rather than constantly needing to move from place to place. In due course, this led to the construction of the world's first big cities, and the emergence of the great ancient civilizations of the world.

This is a neat story. Now let's take a look at what the evidence tells us.

It was once thought that agriculture was 'invented' in the Middle East in the Neolithic period and that it spread around the world thanks to migrants from the area who carried this knowledge with them to other places. But researchers recently uncovered the remains of a 23,000-year-old farming settlement near the Sea of Galilee in Israel, which suggests that farming is actually a lot older than we once thought. Archaeologists have also uncovered large monumental

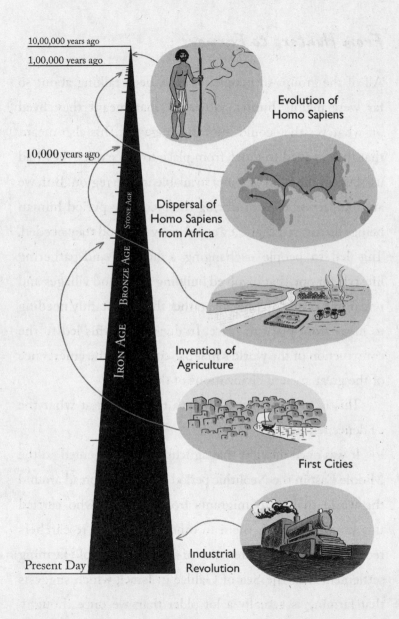

10,00,000 years ago
1,00,000 years ago

Evolution of
Homo Sapiens

10,000 years ago

Dispersal of
Homo Sapiens
from Africa

STONE AGE

BRONZE AGE

IRON AGE

Invention of
Agriculture

First Cities

Present Day

Industrial
Revolution

structures, including one named Göbekli Tepe that was built about 11,500 years ago in south-eastern Turkey, and a stepped pyramid that began to be constructed around the same time in Indonesia. We do not know why they were built, or who built them. In 2001, a team from India's National Institute of Ocean Technology found evidence of sunken settlements while conducting undersea sonar surveys. Since the area was flooded about 7500 years ago, these settlements must have been built before that. It is likely that there are even more such undersea settlements that lie undiscovered.

These monuments and settlements show us evidence of large groups of people working together. We do not yet know whether these were early farming communities or whether they were hunter-gatherer societies. Some researchers have even wondered whether people first began to grow crops in order to feed the people working on these structures. Perhaps it is not simply a coincidence that the wild varieties of wheat from which domesticated wheat was grown were found just a few miles away from Göbekli Tepe.

We also now know that, rather than being invented in one location before spreading elsewhere, both crops and animals began to be domesticated in multiple locations around the world at roughly the same time. Sugar cane was domesticated by the Melanesians on Papua New Guinea. Rice and pigs were domesticated in China. Rice cultivation also spread quickly to South East Asia and India. Sesame and cotton appear to have been first grown in India. West Africans began to grow sorghum and African millet. Cows were domesticated in India and also in the Middle East. And there were even more crops domesticated independently in the Americas. Different people adopted different technologies at different times, and some groups might have skipped a phase or retraced their steps. New discoveries and research are constantly undermining what we thought we knew about the past and teaching us new things about how human beings went from being bands of hunter-gatherers to becoming city dwellers.

One question remains: why did people bother to switch from a life of moving about in search of food to living in one place and growing their food? By all accounts, agriculture did not improve the lives of people. It was a risky business that required a lot of effort without any guarantee that the effort would pay off. The rains could fail, wild animals could destroy crops and neighbouring tribes could come and steal your harvest if you did manage to get one. Moreover, growing your own crops meant you had less variety available to you than hunter-gatherers. And living in close proximity to other people and animals brought with it a greater likelihood of disease spreading. Analysis of human remains from the Neolithic period shows that farmers were less healthy and had shorter lifespans than their hunter-gatherer ancestors. This might explain why the inhabitants of the Ice Age Nile oasis went back to their hunter-gatherer lifestyle as soon as the weather permitted!

Of course, there were some advantages to farming. More calories per unit area could be produced. A settled lifestyle probably also allowed people to have babies more frequently. Populations grew bigger, even though people lived shorter lives.

The (Real) Great Flood

You've probably heard a story or two featuring a great flood. Indians have a legend about Manu, who was warned of the coming of a great flood by the Hindu god Vishnu. In the story, Manu built a large ship and filled it with wise sages, seeds and animals. Vishnu, in the form of a fish, guided Manu to safety. Those on the ship survived the flood and re-established civilization at the foothills of the Himalayas. Does this story sound familiar? That's because it is quite similar to the biblical story of Noah and the Ark! The Sumerian epic of Gilgamesh also mentions a massive flood. The existence of such similar stories across cultures has led to people wondering whether the stories preserve the memory of climate change and coastal flooding that took place around 7000 years ago.

Great floods galore

The Greeks had a myth about a great flood too, as did the Norsemen who lived in Scandinavia. The Greeks believed that the great god Zeus flooded the world because he was angered by the actions of human beings. Only Deucalion, son of the titan Prometheus, and his wife Pyrrha, survived because they had been warned of the flood by Prometheus. Deucalion had built a large wooden chest and filled it with food and other provisions. When the rains came, he and his wife climbed into the chest and floated on the floodwaters and were saved. Interestingly, the story says that the Great Flood changed the landscape of the world.

The last burst of flooding occurred in about 5000 BC and was brought on by climate change and the continued rise in temperatures that had begun after the last Ice Age. In India, the coastline shifted to turn Gujarat's Saurashtra region into a peninsula. Sri Lanka was cut off from the coast of Tamil Nadu and became an island at this time. The islands of Java, Sumatra and Borneo in Indonesia came into being, as the area known as Sundaland became flooded. All of this flooding probably forced people to move. And, even as the rising temperature brought floods to some parts of the world, it was gradually desertifying others. The Sahara, which had been habitable till 7500 years ago, was becoming drier and hotter. The same process occurred in Arabia as well.

These changes made some groups of people take advantage of the warmer climate to move north. By 4500 BC, flooding and desertification had pushed people to settle near the river Nile in Egypt, and the rivers Tigris and Euphrates in Mesopotamia. The Indian subcontinent also saw clusters of human settlement emerge along major rivers. The stage was set for the next big step in human history—civilization.

CHAPTER 2

OF FARMERS, TRADERS AND SHIPS ON THE SEA

Our story now takes us to the evolution of early farming settlements around the world and the relationships that developed between them.

The Very First Farmers

Early excavations in Baluchistan (an area that is now part of Pakistan) suggested that this was the first place in the subcontinent where settlements of people who were growing their own crops came up. Mehrgarh, in the Bolan valley, is the best documented site—people are believed to have lived here from before 6000 BC (that's 8000 years ago!). Here, you can actually see, from the layers of materials in the earth, how people shifted from hunting wild animals for food to rearing domestic ones. The early layers of soil are dominated by the bones of wild animals like gazelle, spotted deer, sambar, blackbuck, nilgai, wild ass and even elephants, while in the later layers, the mix gradually switches to cattle, goat and sheep. Barley was the earliest crop grown here, followed by wheat sometime later.

Recent archaeological finds suggest that farming came up more or less at the same time in a number of other clusters scattered across northern India. For instance, Neolithic farm settlements have been found along the fringes of the Vindhya range in central India, just south of the modern-day city of Prayagraj (formerly Allahabad). Animal bones have also been found in central Indian sites, including those of cattle, deer, goats, wild boar and horses. New Neolithic sites are still being found and excavated, meaning our knowledge of these sites will only keep expanding. As you might remember from the previous chapter, there may also have been even older settlements that are now under the sea, especially off the Gujarat coast.

Agriculture appears to have been adopted a bit later in southern India than in the north. What was the reason behind this? Well, for one thing, hunter-gatherers were not always impressed by farming. It is possible that climatic conditions in the south allowed them to continue living the way they had

Neolithic Farming Settlement

been for years and years, hunting and gathering as needed. Equally interesting is where farming communities were formed when they did come up. We find them concentrated along the river Krishna and its tributary, the Tungabhadra. In contrast, there is very little evidence of early farming settlements along the south-east (i.e., Tamil Nadu and Andhra Pradesh) coast. This is puzzling, as we know that people had been living in these areas for quite a long time. Perhaps the Neolithic sites were washed away by local rivers and covered with silt, or perhaps the settlements existed near the coast and were submerged by changing coastlines.

Cities and Rivers

Around 4500 BC, the savannah grasslands that covered what we now know as the Sahara and the Arabian deserts began to dry out as they had done several thousand years earlier. This once again pushed people to move towards sources of water, such as the Nile in Egypt and the Euphrates and Tigris in Mesopotamia, both of which already had established farming communities. Populations in these areas began to increase, and the need to find a way for everyone to live together in relative peace is possibly what led to the rise of the first kingdoms and states. Mesopotamia saw the rise of Sumerian city states, and by around 3100 BC, Upper and Lower Egypt were unified into a single kingdom with its capital in Memphis.

The Indian subcontinent witnessed the growth of settlements along two major rivers and their tributaries. One of the rivers is the Indus and the other is now the dry riverbed of the Ghaggar. Satellite photos and ground surveys suggest that the Ghaggar was once a mighty river that emerged from the Himalayas near modern-day Chandigarh, then flowed through Haryana, Rajasthan and Sindh before entering the sea through the Rann of Kutch in Gujarat. With the Sutlej and the Yamuna as its tributaries, the river would initially have been as big as the Indus. Strong evidence now suggests that the Ghaggar might be the same as the river Saraswati that is referred to in early Vedic texts.

The Harappan civilization that grew up along the banks of the two rivers went through three phases. The earliest recognizable Harappan site at Bhirrana in Haryana, on the banks of the Ghaggar-Saraswati, has been carbon-dated to 7000 BC. This makes it at least as old as the sites in Baluchistan, which were once considered the oldest in the subcontinent. The early evolution of the settlements in the area is still being analyzed and is not fully understood, but this period coincided with an increase in monsoon rains. From around 5000 BC, the monsoons began to gradually weaken (although they were still much stronger than today). As in Egypt and Mesopotamia, this coincided with more settlements being built along rivers. We know that by 3200 BC, at about the same time that Egypt was being unified, there were a large number of Harappan settlements in both the Ghaggar-Saraswati and the Indus basins.

The second phase, often dubbed the 'mature Harappan period', lasted from 2600 to 2000 BC. This is the period that saw the rise of major cities like Mohenjo-daro, Harappa, Dholavira, Kalibangan and so on. Some of these settlements already existed in the previous phase but they now began to expand. Recent excavations suggest that the largest of these cities was Rakhigarhi in Haryana, which is also in the Ghaggar-Saraswati basin. After 2000 BC, however, the archaeological evidence shows that the prosperity of these communities declined steadily—cities were abandoned, civic management deteriorated and there were signs of economic stress. Some of the settlements struggled on, but the 'late' Harappan period petered out by 1400 BC (this is a simplified timeline and things may have proceeded differently in different settlements).

The Harappans did not build great monuments like the pyramids, but they outmatched their Egyptian and Sumerian peers in terms of population size, the sophistication of their cities and the sheer geographical reach of their civilization. At its height, there were Harappan settlements from Punjab in the north to Gujarat in the south, and from Baluchistan in the west to what is now western Uttar Pradesh in the east. We have even found outposts like Shortughai on the Afghanistan–Tajikistan border and Sutkagen-dor near Pakistan's border with Iran, not far from modern Gwadar.

Dholavira-by-the-Sea

Since this book is about the influence of the Indian Ocean on the history of the world, we will now turn to the Harappan sites that have been uncovered in the Indian state of Gujarat. Before we begin, it is important to have some sense of the landscape in which the Harappans built their settlements. First, western India was much wetter than it is today. Not only was monsoon rain stronger but the Rann of Kutch also received freshwater from both the Ghaggar-Saraswati and the Indus. The estuary of the Indus was much further east than it is today and one of its major channels flowed into Kutch. The fortress of the semi-abandoned town of Lakhpat still stands guard over the channel through which the Indus used to enter the Arabian Sea. Second, the relative sea level during Harappan times was several metres higher than it is today, which means that the Saurashtra peninsula was, at this time, an island. Thus, ships could comfortably sail through what are now the salt flats and marshes of the Rann of Kutch and then make their way out to the Gulf of Khambhat.

Dholavira may look today like it is too far inland to be an effective port but, as shown in the map, it was built on a strategically located island in the third millennium BC. It was accessible by boat from the Arabian Sea to the west as well as the Gulf of Khambhat to the south. Boats from Dholavira would have also been able to sail inland to the cities that were emerging along the riverbanks. In other words, Dholavira would have been important to commerce, as well as possibly being of military importance.

There is evidence that the Ghaggar-Saraswati was already drying up during the early period of Harappan civilization (around 3200 BC). We do not know for certain, but tectonic shifts in northern India may have caused the

Sutlej to shift to the Indus and the Yamuna to the Ganga. There is debate about when exactly this happened, but it is reasonably certain that it happened before the great cities of the mature Harappan period were built.

Why did the Harappans invest in building so many cities along a dying river? Many settlements came up in Gujarat during the mature period, including Lothal, where a large dockyard and sluice gates have been discovered. Next to the dockyard are structures that may have been warehouses and a series of brick platforms where one can imagine stern customs officials inspecting the goods and unscrupulous merchants trying to bribe them. The urban cluster at Dholavira also expanded significantly at this time. The site had a fortified acropolis and a 'lower town'. At some point, the city was expanded to accommodate the growing population, and the old lower town became the 'middle town' and the expanded area became the new lower town. A wooden signboard has been found near one of the gateways. We do not know what it says as the script has not been deciphered.

To Mesopotamia and beyond

There is plenty of evidence that, along with trading within the subcontinent, the Harappans also traded with the Middle East. Merchant ships from Gujarat made their way along the Makran coast, perhaps stopping briefly near Gwadar to visit their outpost at Sutkagen-dor. A bit further west, they would have interacted with the people of the Jiroft civilization, whose archaeological remains have recently been discovered in south-eastern Iran. Although we know very little about the Jiroft people, archaeologists have found seals like those of the Harappans and signs of close cultural links. In particular, several depictions of humped zebu cattle have been found in Bronze Age sites in southern Iran. This is interesting because humped cattle come from India and are commonly seen depicted on Harappan objects.

Some of the Harappans sailing to Iran made their way to Oman as well. Archaeologists digging at Ras al-Junayz, on the easternmost tip of the Arabian Peninsula have found that over 20 per cent of objects were of Harappan origin. Many Harappan merchants also seem to have made their way further into the Persian Gulf to Bahrain, where plenty of Harappan seals, pottery and beads have been found. Harappan-origin artefacts have also been found in ancient Mesopotamian cities like Kish, Nippur and Ur, and the court records of a king in the region refer to ships from Dilmun,

HARAPPAN POTS AND SEALS

Magan and Meluhha (the ancient names used for Bahrain, Oman and the ports of Gujarat/Sindh). There were also land routes that made their way from the northern Harappan cities to Mesopotamia.

Trade with India had a big influence on the Persian Gulf area. Harappan weights and measures became the standard across the region, and locals often copied the Harappan seals. Mesopotamian inscriptions also mention that the Meluhhans were numerous enough to have their own 'villages' or exclusive enclaves in and around Sumerian towns. We do not know for sure what these people were doing there—they could have been a mix of merchants, artisans and mercenaries—but they seem to have been an important part of the bustling economy of Bronze Age Mesopotamia. We also have a handful of references to individuals, including one rowdy Meluhhan who was made to pay ten silver coins to someone called Urur as compensation for breaking his tooth in a brawl!

What kinds of things did the trading ships carry? Well, their cargo holds would have had carnelian beads, weights and measures, different types of wood, pots of ghee (clarified butter) and, most importantly, cotton textiles. The cotton plant was domesticated in India and cotton textiles would remain a major export throughout history. Oddly, we are not sure what the Harappans brought back in exchange. Nothing of obvious Persian Gulf origin has ever been found in any Harappan site, so perhaps they imported perishables like dates and wine. Another possibility is that they imported copper from Oman as the remains of several ancient copper mines have been found there.

Despite the many artefacts they left behind for archaeologists to find, we know surprisingly little about the Harappans themselves. We are not sure what languages they spoke, what gods they worshipped, and their script remains stubbornly undecipherable. We do not even know if their settlements were part of a unified empire or were a network of independent city states that shared a civilization.

Some have tried to find clues about them in an ancient Sanskrit text called the Rig Veda. The Rig Veda is the oldest of Hindu scriptures and was composed in a very archaic form of Sanskrit. It used to be widely believed that the Rig Veda was composed around 1500 BC. It contains ten 'books' of hymns and chants in praise of the gods. Although the text is mostly concerned with religious practice and philosophy, it does make reference to the social and geographical context of those who composed the hymns. The text discusses a part of the subcontinent that it calls the *Sapta Sindhu* or 'Land of the Seven Rivers', which would be the modern-day state of Haryana and a few adjoining parts of Punjab and Rajasthan. This, says the Rig Veda, was the original homeland of the

Bharata tribe that defeated an alliance of ten tribes on the banks of the Ravi in Punjab. They then expanded their empire to the east by defeating a chieftain along the Yamuna.

The text also suggests knowledge of a wider area including the Himalayas in the north, the Ganga on the east, the sea to the south and the rivers of what is now Pakistan's North-West Frontier Province. This roughly coincides with the geographical footprint of the Harappan civilization, which has led some to suggest that the Rig Veda was first composed by the Harappans. The Rig Veda repeatedly mentions the Saraswati River—forty-five hymns are dedicated to the river while the Ganga is barely mentioned twice. One of the hymns clearly places the river between the Yamuna and Sutlej—which is where the dry riverbed of the Ghaggar is located. Importantly, the hymns describe a river in full flow and, unlike later texts, there is no mention of the river drying up. This means that the text must have been written before 2000 BC and most likely before 3200 BC—meaning it may have been a pre-Harappan or early Harappan text.

New information about this period is still flowing in and perhaps a clearer picture may emerge over the next decade.

Interestingly, many of the oldest texts of Zoroastrianism, the religion of ancient Persia (and the Parsi community today), are composed in a language very similar to Vedic

Sanskrit. To this day, the Zoroastrians follow rituals and customs such as the fire sacrifice and the sacred thread that closely resemble Vedic tradition. These and other connections found between the Vedic-era Indians and ancient Iranians have been a source of interest for historians for a very long time. Where do these connections come from? There is strong genetic data that supports the idea that these cultural links reflect the fact that the Iranians and north Indians were part of the same continuum until the Bronze Age.

The location of the Jiroft civilization is particularly intriguing in this context because its sites are in south-east Iran and very close to the westernmost Harappan sites. Given the evidence of trade and use of zebu cattle, they may have been part of an ethnic continuum extending from north-west India. After 2000 BC, as eastern Iran and Baluchistan became increasingly hot and arid, the Jiroft people would have moved west towards Fars province. The ancient name of Fars is *Parsa* and it is here that the Persians emerged as an identifiable people.

The Persians were not the only people with Vedic links in the Middle East. A military elite called the Mitanni came to dominate northern Iraq in the middle of the second millennium BC—their rulers had distinctly Sanskrit-sounding names. Many of their gods also had curiously similar names to Vedic gods. Also, the arrival of the Mitanni in the region witnessed the introduction of a technology of Indian origin—iron. This is five centuries after the earliest mass production of iron took place in southern India, as we will see in the next section. Prior to the arrival of the Mitanni, iron was treated as a precious metal in the Middle East with tiny quantities of meteorite iron being used to make prestige objects in Anatolia (now Turkey). Large-scale extraction from ore was not known. The presence of a Vedic-related people using an Indian technology does suggest that some tribes migrated out of the subcontinent in the second millennium BC.

Christmas or Sol Invictus?

Interestingly, the Indo-Iranian god Mitra was also popular with the citizens of the Roman Empire, who knew him as the solar god Mithras. The pagan Romans used to celebrate a big festival called Saturnalia that went on for a week from 17 December. At the end of the festival, on 25 December, the Mithras cult would celebrate the feast of Sol Invictus or 'the Unconquered Sun'. Many scholars believe that when the Christians came to dominate the Roman Empire, they simply took over the popular pagan festival (after all, the actual birthdate of Jesus Christ is not known). Mind you, not everyone agreed with this choice and the Orthodox Church still celebrates Christmas on 7 January. Nevertheless, the 25 December holiday has survived as a day of festivity for most Christians and even non-Christians.

Climate Change, Early Edition

The great Harappan cities flourished till around 2000 BC when there was a sudden deterioration in economic and social conditions. It has now been confirmed by a series of studies that this was due to a shift in climate that also seems to have affected other Bronze Age civilizations. The change in weather patterns seems to have also affected Egypt and Mesopotamia, and it caused great economic and political disruption. Iran's Jiroft civilization died out and was forgotten. Egypt's Old Kingdom collapsed and the country went back to being divided into Upper Egypt and Lower Egypt. In Mesopotamia, the Akkadian Empire also collapsed around 2100 BC. North-west India probably experienced something similar as monsoon rains failed.

There is evidence that the Harappans tried to adapt by switching from crops like wheat and barley to crops like millets, which needed less water. The problem was that the new crops had smaller yields that could only support small rural communities but not large urban centres. The great Harappan cities could not be fed any more, and they were abandoned one by one as people migrated in search of water. These migrations show up in the changes we can study through genetics. The ANI and ASI populations suddenly go through a period of rapid mixing from around 2100 BC onward. It is possible that this mixing was quickened by some ASI groups moving north at the same time that the ANI were moving south and east. The mixing of these two genetic pools is responsible for the bulk of India's present-day population. Genetic markers also suggest that this mixing went on for more than 2000 years, so much so that there are no 'pure' ANI and ASI any more. After all this blending, the majority of Indians are most closely related to each other irrespective of their ancient origins.

The migration of Harappans to the east and south would have spread their technologies and culture to these areas. In the past, historians assumed that the Harappans brought their ideas to the east, south and then onward to South East Asia. The reality is that there were already established populations and possibly even cities in the areas where the Harappans settled (a preliminary study hints that the city of Varanasi may be as old as the Harappan cities). New findings in the Gangetic plains suggest that there was an old civilization already in place when the Harappans were abandoning their cities. A site called Sanauli in Uttar Pradesh has yielded objects such as a chariot, swords, shield and a warrior's helmet. Thus, plenty of influence flowed in reverse and Indian civilization is the result of a messy process where people, ideas and influences flowed in multiple directions.

Interestingly, the people living in southern India may not have built sophisticated cities in the Bronze Age but it is they who initiated the Iron Age. The traditional view is that iron was introduced to India by invaders from Central Asia. Archaeological finds over the last two decades suggest instead that, in fact, India was probably where iron was first mass produced. Initially, the evidence pointed to the earliest use of the metal around the eighteenth century BC in the middle Gangetic plains, but now it appears that it originated much further south and at a much earlier period. Students of the University of Hyderabad made a startling discovery in 2014–15 while conducting excavations on their campus. They found a number of iron artefacts, including weapons, that dated from around 2400–1800 BC. This is arguably the oldest systematic use of iron in the world!

The Land of Punt

The collapse of the major Bronze Age cities around 2000 BC affected the thriving trade route between the Persian Gulf and India's western coast. However, there is an interesting piece of evidence to show that the links between these regions did not entirely disappear: the discovery of black peppercorns stuffed up the nostrils of the mummy of Pharaoh Ramses II. While we do not know if this condemned the pharaoh to frequent sneezing in the afterlife, it shows that the Indian Ocean trade networks of the thirteenth century BC were capable of transporting pepper from its origin in south-western India to Egypt. Since it is unlikely that sailors of this period could directly cross the Arabian Sea, the spice was probably shipped up the coast from Kerala to Gujarat, and then along the Makran coast to Oman. From here, there were two possibilities. It could have continued along the old Persian Gulf route to Mesopotamia and then overland to Egypt. However, it is just as possible that pepper made its way south from Oman to Yemen and Eritrea, a region that the ancient Egyptians called the Land of Punt.

We know that the ancient Egyptians sailed down the Red Sea on frequent trading expeditions to the Land of Punt. One of the expeditions is depicted on a panel at the memorial temple of Queen Hatshepsut who ruled Egypt between 1473 and 1458 BC. Hatshepsut is a fascinating character—a female pharaoh who ruled in her own name. There are other female rulers in Egyptian history, but she overshadows them in terms of the scale of her building projects, her military victories and, of course, her ambitious maritime expedition to the Land of Punt. The temple panels depict large galleys with sails, oars and stern-side paddles for steering. They probably embarked from Wadi Gawasis on Egypt's Red Sea coast and sailed down the Red Sea to what is now Yemen and Eritrea. The expedition would return with gold, ivory, different kinds of wood, exotic animals and, most importantly, frankincense.

What's that smell?

Frankincense was a very valuable product of ancient Yemen and Oman. It is the dried resin of a thorny tree and gives off a pleasant smell when burnt. It was widely used in religious ceremonies and is one of the gifts that the 'three wise men' are said to have brought for the baby Jesus. Even today, anyone visiting the Yemen–Oman coast will find it commonly sold in traditional markets and the smell of burning frankincense pervades shops, restaurants and homes.

Who were the people who lived in the Land of Punt? Today we think of the Yemeni as being Arab, but till the advent of Islam, south-eastern Arabia was home to a number of related but constantly feuding tribes such as the Himyar, the Hadramawt and the Sabeans. Archaeologists have found as many as 10,000 inscriptions describing the lives, feuds, treaties and rulers of these tribes. The Sabeans were one of the most powerful tribes. Around the eighth century BC, they created an empire that extended from into Eritrea and parts of Ethiopia. The Sabeans may have introduced wheat and barley to Ethiopia, and also introduced their script, which was originally written left-to-right and right-to-left on alternate lines; not such a silly idea if you think about it. The Sabean script would evolve into the Ge'ez script of the kingdom of Aksum and survives as the modern Ethiopian script (although it is now written exclusively left-to-right).

These early interactions between the Yemenis and the Egyptians would later extend to neighbouring lands and probably gave rise to the legend about King Solomon and Queen Sheba (i.e., Saba). According to the Ethiopian version of the legend, when Queen Sheba returned after meeting Solomon in Jerusalem, she gave birth to a child named David. This child would grow up to be King Menelik I, founder of the Solomonic dynasty of Aksum. Although there is no historical evidence supporting this story about Solomon, Sheba, Menelik and the stealing of the Ark, it has been part of the national founding myth of Ethiopia since the medieval Solomonic dynasty came to power in AD 1262. The royal dynasty promoted the story as having a biblical lineage was one way for the dynasty to show it had the right to rule.

Looking to the East

With all the migrating and churning going on in the western Indian Ocean rim, one adventurous band of people from the subcontinent decided to head east. They seem to have sailed along the eastern coast, past Sumatra and Java and eventually ended up in Australia. Recent genetic studies show that a bit more than 4000 years ago, a band of people from the Indian subcontinent turned up in Australia and contributed their DNA to the aborigines. This finding confounds the earlier belief that there were no new arrivals to the island continent between the initial migration of Melanesians 45,000 years ago and the arrival of the Europeans. Moreover, the new immigrants brought their pets along, which were the ancestors of the dingo. This is possibly why this Australian wild dog looks suspiciously like the stray dogs one sees all over India.

As mentioned in the previous chapter, the coastlines of South East Asia witnessed major changes as Sundaland was inundated by the post-Ice Age floods. Recent genetic studies confirm that the region's current population landscape is heavily influenced by human migrations following the floods. These South East Asian migrations involved two major ethnic groups—the Austronesians and the Austroasiatic. To make it less confusing, let's call them AN and AA respectively. The AN included the ancestors of the Malays, Indonesians, Filipinos, Bruneians, Timorese and significant minorities in neighbouring countries. It also includes Taiwanese aborigines and the Polynesians spread across the Pacific. As one can see, they had a strong maritime culture.

It was once thought that this group originated in Taiwan, but it now appears that they lived along the eastern coast of Sundaland and were forced by the floods to search for new homes. The outrigger canoe was an important part of their maritime culture. It is a simple design but clearly very effective as it allowed the AN to settle most of the islands in South East Asia during the Neolithic period. Some of these islands may have had existing Melanesian populations who seem to have been squeezed into a smaller area in and around New Guinea and Fiji. A few centuries later, the eastern Polynesian branch of ANs would set out to colonize a swathe of islands across the Pacific—from New Zealand to Hawaii and Easter Island. Similarly, the western branch would sail across the Indian Ocean and settle in Madagascar. Thus the AN came to colonize a large swathe of the planet from Madagascar to Hawaii.

The speakers of AA languages were the other important ethnic group of South East Asia. They include the Vietnamese, Khmer (i.e., Cambodian) and the Mon in Myanmar and Thailand. Unlike their Malay and Polynesian cousins, however, this group seems to have preferred to migrate over land rather than via the sea. At some point, small groups of AAs drifted into north-east India. The descendants of these migrations are the Munda-speaking tribes, such as the Santhals, who are scattered all over eastern and central India. A somewhat later wave survives today as the Khasis of the state of Meghalaya. Thus India's population mix includes people who speak languages related to Vietnamese and Khmer.

Matrilineal customs, or the tracing of familial relationships and inheritance of property through the maternal or mother's line, rather than the father's, appear to have been an important feature of the AA-speaking groups migrating across South East Asia and into India's north-east. The Khasis of Meghalaya, for instance, remain matrilineal to this day. Traces of matrilineal customs seem to have been imbibed even by neighbouring communities that may never have been matrilineal. For instance, in Assamese Hindu weddings, the sindoor (red vermilion) is applied to the forehead of the bride by the mother-in-law in the 'jurun' ceremony that precedes the wedding. The act of applying sindoor is a key part of Hindu marriage rituals and is usually reserved for the husband. The performance of this rite by the groom's mother symbolizes the women of the family accepting a new member—a very matrilineal view of a wedding.

But why were the AAs matrilineal in the first place? The answer to this riddle is found in the study of the genetics of the AA groups. It appears that the Indian branch is the result of almost exclusively male migrations. At the risk of oversimplifying, one could say that groups like the Santhals and Khasis are the result of male migrants from South East Asia marrying local women. We do not know exactly what drove these migrations, but this movement was not quite one of conquest since the incoming males seem to have accepted the property rights of the local women.

CHAPTER 3

ALEXANDER, ASHOKA AND KHARAVELA

By 1300 BC, the use of iron had become commonplace across north and central India, and it was during the Iron Age that two major highways came to connect the subcontinent. The first was an east–west road called the Uttara Path (Northern Road) that ran from eastern Afghanistan, across the Gangetic plains to the ports of Bengal. This road would be repaired and rebuilt throughout Indian history and survives today as National Highway 1 between Amritsar and Delhi and as National Highway 2 between Delhi and Kolkata. The second was a north–south highway called the Dakshina Path (Southern Road). This was more like a tangled network that started around the Prayagraj–Varanasi section of the Gangetic plains and made its way in a south-westerly direction to Ujjain. Here it split into two with one branch going to the ports of Gujarat and the other branch making its way further south via Pratishthana (modern Paithan) to Kishkindha in Karnataka and beyond.

We now move forward through history, through the Iron Age. During this time, conquerors came and went, groups of people migrated and branched off, and dynasties began and ended.

Our Neighbours, the Lion People

Archaeologists have found remnants of a possible river port at a place called Golbai Sasan in Odisha that date back to 2300 BC. The remains of many ancient ports have also been found all along the coast between the westernmost mouth of the Ganga and Chilika lake. The river connected the seaports to the kingdoms of the interior while the lake, which has an outlet to the sea, acted as a safe harbour. What we know for certain is that there was a distinct boom in coastal trade from around 800 BC. At the heart of this was the region called Kalinga (roughly modern-day Odisha) as well as parts of the modern-day state of West Bengal.

These ancient mariners were not capable of sailing directly across the Indian Ocean at this early stage. Instead, they would have hugged the shore and traded their way down the Andhra and Tamil coast. At some stage, they seem to have sailed across to Sri Lanka and begun to settle there.

The story of the *Mahavamsa*

The *Mahavamsa*, an epic written in the ancient language Pali, tells a story about how the Sinhalese came to Sri Lanka. It is said that at the beginning of the sixth century BC, the king of Vanga (i.e., Bengal) had a beautiful daughter who was kidnapped by a powerful lion. The lion kept the princess imprisoned in a cave, and she eventually gave birth to a son and a daughter. The son, Sinhabahu, grew up to be a strong young man. One day, when the lion was away, he broke open the cave-prison and escaped with his mother and sister. The lion pursued them, but after several adventures, Sinhabahu faced his father and finally killed him. Sinhabahu then established a kingdom and built a capital city Sinhapura. Many years passed and Sinhabahu had a son called Vijaya, who turned out to be a violent lout and a disgrace to the family. After hearing repeated complaints from his subjects, King Sinhabahu eventually decided to banish Vijaya and 700 of his supporters. So, Vijaya sailed south and landed in Sri Lanka. He faced some resistance from the locals, presumably the Vedda, led by a woman called Kuveni. However, Vijaya prevailed and established his kingdom. The *Mahavamsa* tells us that King Vijaya now gave up his earlier erratic behaviour, married a Tamil princess from the Pandya clan and ruled his kingdom responsibly for thirty-eight years.

Genetic studies have confirmed that the island was already inhabited by the ancestors of the Vedda, a small tribe that has long been suspected of being the original inhabitants. They are probably descendants of people who migrated here before the Great Flood cut them off from the mainland. The migrants from Kalinga, however, would soon become the dominant population—the Sinhalese.

The Sinhalese link to eastern India matches genetic, linguistic and cultural evidence and survives in many little ways. For example, the lion is an important symbol of the Sinhalese people; their name literally means 'the lion people'. Odisha remains a major centre for the worship of Narasimha (the god Vishnu in the form of a half-lion, half-man). The town of Puri is famous for the temple of Jagannath, another form of Vishnu, but also has a very ancient temple to Narasimha, and there are several rituals where the latter is given precedence to this day. Similarly, in Bengal, the goddess Durga is almost always depicted riding a lion. Perhaps the lion on the Sri Lankan flag and Durga's lion share the same cultural origins?

Herodotus and the Giant Ants of India

At the same time that people from Kalinga were settling in Sri Lanka, a Greek historian called Herodotus was writing a remarkable book, *The Histories*, which is the first known attempt to systematically research and write a historical narrative. Like a modern-day researcher, Herodotus weighed the evidence for himself and often disbelieved what he was told. In his book, he gives us a glimpse of what the people of the Mediterranean thought of the world of the Indian Ocean, which the ancient Greeks called the Erythraean Sea. The Persian Achaemenid Empire of this period stretched from Egypt to the western bank of the Indus, and was a constant threat to the independence of the Greek city states. Since a large contingent of soldiers from the subcontinent was part of the Persian imperial army, Herodotus seems to have been familiar with the inhabitants of this part of the world.

The Histories tells us that these soldiers wore cotton clothes, carried bows and used arrows made of cane and tipped with iron. We are also told that they had horses and chariots. But Herodotus's knowledge of these soldiers' homeland is a garbled mix of fact and fiction from many sources. He is aware that India is a large and populous place where numerous languages are spoken. He also recounts a Persian expedition that sailed down the Indus and made its way to Egypt through the Red Sea. This was probably an established trade route by this time. It seems to have been commercially important enough for Herodotus to have referred to a canal being built to connect the Red Sea to the Nile—an early Suez Canal! The Greeks also seemed to believe that India was the easternmost inhabited land and that there were only oceans and deserts beyond it.

Among many other fantastical stories, Herodotus recounts the method by which, according to him, the people of India mined gold. There was said to be a sandy desert in India inhabited by giant ants 'in size somewhat smaller than dogs, but bigger than foxes'. When these ants burrowed their nests into the ground, they dug out sand that was rich in gold. People made their way into the desert on camels to collect the sand in the midday sun. However, the ants were dangerous and one had to collect the sand quickly and escape. We are categorically told that female camels were faster than the males, and should be preferred for the operation as there was some risk of the ants chasing after the gold-diggers. Now, this is the kind of useful information one should always remember if one wants to avoid being eaten alive by rampaging giant ants!

PHOENICIAN SHIP

The Phoenicians did it first (or did they?)

The Phoenicians lived along the eastern Mediterranean coast, from about 1500 BC until about 300 BC. They were famous for their skill as seafarers in the ancient world. The fleet was said to have set out from the Red Sea and sailed down the coast of East Africa. At this stage, they may not have been in entirely unfamiliar territory as Herodotus suggests that the Phoenicians had migrated to the Mediterranean from the Indian Ocean rim. In autumn, they went ashore and sowed a tract of land with corn. Having replenished their food stocks with the harvest, they set sail again, and in this way, made it back to the Mediterranean through the Strait of Gibraltar after three years. If true, this expedition would suggest that the ancients had gone around the Cape of Good Hope a good 2000 years before Vasco da Gama! Herodotus, however, did not believe the story because of a minor detail—the Phoenicians insisted that when they made the turn at the bottom of Africa, the sun was to their right. Herodotus thought that this claim was just too absurd, but we know that this is exactly what one should expect south of the Tropic of Capricorn.

Alexander of Macedon and the Rise of the Mauryan Empire

The history of the ancient Greek city states is dominated by their conflicts with the Persian Empire, the superpower of that time. This rivalry culminated in a large-scale

Greek–Macedonian invasion led by Alexander III of Macedon, better known as Alexander the Great. After winning a series of battles in the Levant (roughly in the region of present-day Syria and Lebanon) and conquering Egypt, Alexander's army decisively defeated the Persians led personally by their ruler, Darius III, in 331 BC at Gaugamela (near modern Mosul, northern Iraq). The Roman-era historian Arrian mentions a contingent of horsemen from India that fought for the Persian cause and continued to put up a fierce resistance even after Darius had fled the battlefield.

Alexander now controlled the Persian Empire, but his dream was to conquer the whole known world. Thus, in the winter of 327–326 BC, he led his army through Afghanistan towards India. Along the way he subdued several small kingdoms before marching into the plains of Punjab, where he and his local allies defeated the Indian king, Porus. Alexander wanted to keep pushing east, but his troops were weary and wanted to go home. There were also rumours of a large army being mobilized by the Nandas of Magadh (roughly modern Bihar). The conqueror was forced by a near-rebellion to change plans. He decided to return home by sailing down the Indus in the mistaken belief that the river became the Nile in its lower reaches. In other words, the Macedonians thought that if they simply sailed down the Indus, they would end up in the Mediterranean. It is possible that they misunderstood Herodotus's account of the Persian expedition that sailed down the Indus and then made its way to Egypt through the Red Sea.

ALEXANDER VS PORUS

Whatever the real reason for the decision, Alexander's army pillaged their way down the Indus till they arrived on the shores of the Arabian Sea in 325 BC. The main channel of the river used to flow much further east of its current location and it is likely that the Macedonians reached the sea near Lakhpat in Kutch. Having realized his mistake, Alexander sent back part of the army by sea following the old Harappan coastal route to the Persian Gulf. However, perhaps due to the lack of boats, he marched the bulk of his army through the deserts of Baluchistan and eastern Iran. It was a very bad choice and thousands of soldiers died from hunger and thirst in the stark, barren landscape. Much of the plunder from years of campaigning had to be abandoned as most of the pack animals died. Alexander's army arrived in Mesopotamia undefeated but decimated. Alexander died soon after his return to Babylon, possibly poisoned by members of the Macedonian elite who had come to fear his increasingly erratic behaviour. His young son was later murdered and the generals divided up the empire among themselves.

Alexander's brief excursion to the Indian subcontinent had one unintended, but important, consequence. A scholar called Chanakya and his protégé Chandragupta Maurya took advantage of the political confusion caused by the invasion to carve out a power base in India's north-west. After several attempts, they defeated the Nanda king of Magadh and created the foundations for the powerful Mauryan Empire. In 305 BC, Chandragupta defeated Seleucus Nikator, the general who had taken over most of Alexander's Asian possessions. The treaty between Seleucus and Chandragupta handed the Indians a large chunk of territory extending into present-day Afghanistan and Baluchistan. One of Seleucus's daughters was also given in marriage to a Mauryan prince, perhaps Chandragupta himself or his son Bindusara. Seleucus, in return, received a gift of 500 Indian war elephants and their mahouts.

What happened to the elephants?

In case you were wondering what Seleucus did with his elephants, here is what happened to them. In 301 BC, Seleucus fought in the Battle of Ipsus. He used his elephants against rival generals and established himself as the most powerful of Alexander's successors. Thereafter, elephants became the symbol of the Seleucid Empire and Seleucus was often depicted on coins seated on elephant-drawn chariots.

Chandragupta abdicated in 298 BC (or 303 BC according to another source) in favour of his son Bindusara who ruled till 273 BC. Bindusara had inherited an empire that was already very large—from Afghanistan to Bengal. He seems to have extended the realm further south until the empire covered all but the southern tip of the peninsula. His reign seems to have been largely peaceful, except for a few rebellions. Bindusara also seems to have maintained diplomatic and trade links with the kingdoms carved out from Alexander's empire.

The establishment of the Mauryan Empire across the subcontinent would have led to a spurt in internal trade along both the northern and southern routes. In his treatise *Arthashastra*, Chanakya (also called Kautilya) has left us his opinion on the relative merits of trading along the Uttara Path and the Dakshina Path. The text tells us that earlier scholars had a preference for the northern highway, but Chanakya makes the case that the southern route was a much better source of all goods besides horses and woollen cloth. Perhaps this reflects the changing economic dynamics of the subcontinent by the fourth century BC. Chanakya specifically mentions diamonds, a gemstone that was at that time only found in peninsular India; it was a by-product of the volcanic processes that created the Deccan plateau.

Meanwhile, maritime trade continued to flourish. Ships would have sailed out of the ports of Gujarat and sailed along the Makran coast to the Persian Gulf, while some would have

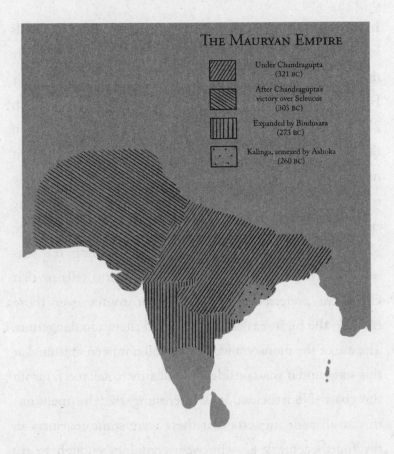

THE MAURYAN EMPIRE

Under Chandragupta
(321 BC)

After Chandragupta's
victory over Seleucus
(305 BC)

Expanded by Bindusara
(273 BC)

Kalinga, annexed by Ashoka
(260 BC)

made their way into the Red Sea. We know that Bindusara
was in touch with Alexander's successors in the Middle
East. He once asked Seleucus's successor Antiochus for figs,
wine and a Greek philosopher. Antiochus sent the figs and
the wine but politely refused to send the philosopher on the
grounds that Greek law forbade the sale of scholars! So, what
did Bindusara send in return? We know that Antiochus used

Indian war elephants to fend off a major invasion by Gauls into Anatolia (modern-day Turkey). So it is quite likely that he was being supplied elephants and their mahouts by Bindusara. Ashoka, who ruled after Bindusara's death in 274 BC, also maintained the links with the Greek rulers of the Middle East. His thirteenth edict mentions that he sent missionaries as far as Syria, Egypt and Macedonia. Maritime trade was also active along the eastern coast and the same edict mentions the Cholas and Pandyas of the Tamil country.

Despite all these maritime linkages, sailing the seas was still dangerous business. The *Arthashastra* tells us that Chanakya preferred coastal and river routes over those crossing the high seas as he considered them too dangerous. The use of the monsoon winds had still not been mastered at this stage and it was considered foolhardy to sail too far from the coast. Nonetheless, it is interesting that he mentions this at all as it suggests that there were some mariners in the fourth century BC who were confident enough to try transoceanic routes.

Ashoka the Bloodthirsty and the Kingdom of Kalinga

In 274 BC, Bindusara suddenly fell ill and died. The crown prince, Sushima, was away fending off incursions on the north-western frontiers and rushed back to the imperial capital Pataliputra (present-day Patna) when he heard the news. However, on arrival he found that Ashoka, one of his half-brothers, had taken control of the city with the help of Greek mercenaries. Ashoka, it seems, had Sushima killed at the eastern gates. Four years of bloody civil war followed, in which Ashoka seems to have killed all male rivals in his family as well as hundreds of loyalist officials. Having consolidated his power, he was finally crowned emperor in 270 BC.

All accounts agree that Ashoka was brutal and unpopular in the early years of his reign. The story of what happened after usually goes like this: Ashoka invaded Kalinga, was shocked by the death and destruction, converted to Buddhism and became a pacifist. But let us look at what evidence there is to support this story. Ashoka invaded Kalinga in 262 BC, but some minor rock edicts suggest that Ashoka had converted to Buddhism more than two years before the invasion. Interestingly, no Buddhist text links his conversion to the war. Moreover, he seems to have had links with Buddhists for a decade before his conversion. So it is possible that his conversion to Buddhism may have had more to do with politics than with regret over the pain and suffering of war.

Also, it is usually thought that the Kalinga that Ashoka invaded was an independent kingdom, but there is some reason to believe that it was actually a rebellious province or a vassal that was no longer trusted. We know that the Nandas, who preceded the Mauryas, had already conquered Kalinga. Therefore, it is likely that it became part of the Mauryan Empire when Chandragupta took over the Nanda kingdom. In any case, it seems strange that a large and expansionist empire like that of the Mauryas would have tolerated an independent state so close to its capital Pataliputra and its main port at Tamralipti. So it is likely that Kalinga would not have been an entirely independent kingdom under Bindusara—it was either a province or a close vassal, and something happened during the early years of Ashoka's reign to shake the status quo. Perhaps Kalinga had sided with Ashoka's rivals during the battle for succession or declared itself independent in the confusion of those times.

Whatever the reason for Ashoka's ire, a large Mauryan army marched into Kalinga around 262 BC. It is believed that the two armies met on the banks of the River Daya at Dhauli near modern Bhubaneswar, but recent archaeological excavations point to a place called Yuddha Meruda being the site of the main battle. This was followed by a desperate and bloody last stand at the Kalingan capital of Tosali. The site is at a place called Radhanagar, a couple of hours' drive from Cuttack. It is situated in a broad fertile plain watered by the Brahmani River and surrounded by low hills.

The remains of the city's earthwork defences suggest that Tosali was built in the middle of the plains. Archaeologists have only excavated a small section of the walls but have found it riddled with arrowheads; a blizzard of arrows must have been unleashed by the Mauryan army. The Kalingans never stood a chance. Ashoka's own inscriptions tell us that 1,00,000 died in the war and an even larger number died from wounds and hunger. A further 1,50,000 were taken away as captives. Ashoka, it is often argued, was horrified by his own brutality and became a Buddhist and a pacifist.

But, as we have seen, he may already have been a practising Buddhist by then. Besides, the main evidence of his repentance comes from his own inscriptions, and only those in locations far away from Odisha (such as in Shahbazgarhi in north-western Pakistan). None of the inscriptions in Odisha express any remorse.

The Ashokan inscriptions at Dhauli are engraved on a rock at the base of a hill. What will strike anyone reading them is how they specifically leave out any sign of regret. If Ashoka was genuinely remorseful, he would surely have made this clear to the very people whom he had wronged? But even the seemingly regretful inscriptions include a clear threat of further violence against other groups like the forest tribes. Many of the inscriptions are placed in locations where the average citizen or official of that time would not have been able to read them.

ASHOKAN EDICT
AT DHAULI

Is it possible that some of the inscriptions were really meant for later generations rather than his contemporaries? Was Ashoka using his inscriptions as a tool of political propaganda to counter his reputation for cruelty?

The Buddhist text, the *Ashokavadana*, tells of Ashoka's violence towards the Jain and Ajivika sects even after his supposed turn to pacifism. In addition to such alleged acts of cruelty, an increasingly unwell Ashoka watched his empire disintegrate from rebellion, internal family squabbles and fiscal stress in his later years. While he was still alive, the empire had probably lost all the north-western territories that had been acquired from Seleucus. Within a few years of Ashoka's death in 232 BC, the Satvahanas had taken over most of the territories in southern India and Kalinga too had seceded. His legacy, therefore, seems to have been a mixed one.

Was he a great king or a cruel and unpopular usurper who presided over the disintegration of a large and well-functioning empire built by his father and grandfather? At the very least, it seems that Ashoka was some shade of grey at best.

Kharavela's Revenge

Ashoka's successors tried hard to stabilize the empire after his death and tried to mend relations across groups.

Ashoka's immediate successor was Dasharatha who reached out to the Ajivikas and constructed the rock-cut Nagarjuni and Barabar caves near Gaya for the sect. After Dasharatha, the empire seems to have broken up rapidly. Meanwhile, the Satvahanas began to take over the southern territories of the empire. They seem to have been from Andhra country and called themselves the 'Andhra-bhritya' or servants of the Andhras. The modern Indian state of Andhra Pradesh is named after them. The Satvahanas set up their capital at Pratishthana, in present-day Maharashtra, a major node on the southern highway, and took on the title 'Lords of Dakshina Path'.

As the Satvahanas expanded north, they came in conflict with the Indo-Greeks and Sakas (Scythians) who had taken over north-western India and were now trying to take control of the ports of Gujarat. An inscription in Nasik tells us of the Satvahana king Gautamiputra Satakarni who defeated and pushed back the Greeks and Scythians. The invaders, however, seem to have met with less resistance from the later Mauryans and we see them making raids deeper and deeper into the Gangetic plains. Taking advantage of the situation, Kalinga rebelled and seceded under the leadership of the Chedi clan.

Around 193 BC, a remarkable military leader called Kharavela came to the throne of Kalinga. We know about him because of a long inscription at Hathigumpha, or Elephant's Cave near Bhubaneswar. We are told that, in the early years of his reign, Kharavela led a large army against the Satvahanas and secured his western frontiers. Around 185 BC, he seems to have marched north into Magadh, where he defeated the invading Indo-Greek king Demetrius and forced him to retreat to Mathura, possibly at the behest of the Mauryans. Kharavela realized that the old Mauryan Empire was on its last legs and, four years later, he returned with a large army and sacked the Mauryan capital. He tells us proudly that he brought back the Jain idols that had been taken away to Pataliputra at the time of the Nanda kings and that he made King Bahasatimita (probably the last Mauryan king Brihadhrata) bow to him. With the prestige of the Mauryas in tatters, the last emperor would be deposed by his own general Pushyamitra Sunga.

Ashoka's brutal invasion had taken place only three generations earlier and would have still been fresh in the memory of Kalinga. So, when Kharavela returned from his Magadh campaign, he had his exploits inscribed on a rock on Udayagiri hill, now effectively a suburb of Bhubaneswar. The hill has a number of beautifully carved caves cut into the hillside for the use of Jain monks. Archaeologists have recently uncovered a large fortified city from this period at Sishupalgarh, very close to modern Bhubaneswar. It is very likely the remains of Kharavela's capital, Kalinga-nagari.

Kharavela's inscriptions suggest that he had defeated the Satvahanas, the Mauryas, the Indo-Greeks and even the Pandyas of Tamil country in the deep south. Kharavela's inscriptions are mostly about his military campaigns, but there are a few references to economic concerns. The restoration of a number of reservoirs and the extension of an old Nanda-era canal are mentioned. The management of water supply was obviously an important activity expected of the state. There is also a fleeting mention of the king gifting Chinese silk to priests/monks. This would suggest that Indian merchants operating in South East Asia had connected to trade routes that extended all the way to China.

We now turn to their exploits.

CHAPTER 4

TRADERS FROM THE WEST AND TRAVELLERS GOING EAST

The period following the collapse of the Mauryan Empire saw a boom in economic activity and mercantile trade. Merchant ships set sail from Satvahana and Kalinga ports, as well as those of the small kingdoms in the far south, to trade as far as Egypt in the west and Vietnam in the east. These ships carried goods to trade in exchange for a variety of items that they brought back, but they also facilitated the exchange of something more intangible and perhaps even more lasting than cotton, silk or wine: ideas.

The Brahmin and the Princess

As you already know, Odiya–Bengali seafarers had been visiting and settling in Sri Lanka from the sixth century BC.

At some point, these sailors also began to trade with South East Asia. In the initial phase, they did not have the confidence to sail directly across the Bay of Bengal. Instead, they hugged the coast till the Isthmus of Kra (the thin strip of land, now part of Thailand, from which the Malay Peninsula hangs). The goods they brought were then taken overland to the Gulf of Thailand, where they were loaded again on ships destined for ports in Cambodia and southern Vietnam. From the Mekong delta in Vietnam, merchandise would be traded up the coast to China. This route helps explain why traders from India's eastern coast established links with faraway Vietnam before they began trading with the Indonesian islands of Java and Bali, which might appear closer on a map.

It is in the Mekong delta that we witness the establishment of the first 'Indianized' kingdom of South East Asia around the first century BC. The Chinese called it the kingdom of Funan. There is an interesting legend about how this kingdom was founded. It is said that a merchant ship from India was sailing through the region when it was attacked by pirates led by Soma, the daughter of the chieftain of the local Naga clan. The Indians fought back and fended off the attackers led by a handsome young Brahmin called Kaundinya.

Unfortunately, the ship had been damaged and had to be beached for repairs. The merchants must have been worried about a second attack but luck turned in their favour. It appears Princess Soma was so impressed by Kaundinya's bravery that she had fallen in love! She proposed marriage and the offer was accepted. This union is said to have founded a lineage that ruled Funan for many generations. We have no way of knowing if this legend is based on true events, but slightly different versions of the story are repeated in inscriptions by both the Chams of Vietnam and the Khmers of Cambodia—the royal families of both claim descent from Soma and Kaundinya. It is also repeated in Chinese records from the period.

Islands of Gold and Grain

By the end of the second century BC, Indian mariners appear to have learnt enough about the monsoon winds and ocean currents to attempt a more southern route across the Indian Ocean to the islands of Indonesia. Odisha's Lake Chilika, a large brackish lake with a small opening to the sea, was an important starting point for this voyage. The ships did not set sail directly for Indonesia. Instead, they used the north-eastern monsoon winds that blow from mid-November to sail down the coast to Sri Lanka. This was already a well-known route, and the merchants probably stopped along the way to trade as well. In Sri Lanka, the ships would have taken on freshwater and supplies before using ocean currents to cross the Indian Ocean to the northern tip of Sumatra (called Suvarnadweep, or Island of Gold in Sanskrit texts). From here, the ships could choose to sail down the Strait of Malacca towards Palembang and take the sea route to Borneo and Vietnam. Alternatively, they could head south hugging the western coast of Sumatra to Bali and Java (given the name Yavadweep, or Island of Barley/Grain in Sanskrit texts).

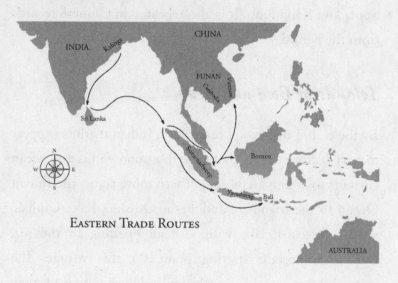

EASTERN TRADE ROUTES

After finishing their purchases and sales, most ships would have used the countercurrent to return to Sri Lanka, and then Odisha. If the sailors had set out from Odisha in mid-November, it is estimated that they would have reached the islands of Java/Bali by mid-January. They would then have had two months to conduct their business before they began their return journey in mid-March. This would allow them to get back to Sri Lanka in time to catch the early south-west monsoon winds in May that would take them home.

The merchants of Kalinga were not the only ones making the journey to Indonesia. There were merchants from the Tamil, Andhra and Bengal coasts sailing there too. There were even horse-traders from India's north-west who made their way to the port of Tamralipti in Bengal and then sailed to Java and Sumatra. However, in the initial phase, it is the Sadhaba merchants of Kalinga who seem to have had a dominant influence.

The most important Indian export at this time was cotton textiles, which would continue to be in much demand across the Indian Ocean rim till modern times. Excavations in South East Asia have unearthed hoards of carnelian beads and a variety of metalware. By the first century AD, we find that Indian merchants were also bringing Mediterranean and West Asian products that they had purchased from the Romans, Greeks and Arabs. Artefacts found in Sembiran in Bali show that they had links with Arikamedu, an Indo-Roman port situated just outside Puducherry.

But what did these ancient traders take back with them? We know that Chinese silks, via ports in Vietnam, and camphor from Sumatra, were transported home. The islands of Indonesia would have been a source of cloves, nutmeg and other spices. Many of the spices thought to be 'Indian' by medieval Europeans actually came from Indonesia—except black pepper, which grows along the south-western coast of India. Until the late eighteenth century, the world's entire supply of cloves came from the tiny islands of Ternate and Tidore in the Maluku group!

Trade links with South East Asia unsurprisingly led to cultural exchange: we have evidence of the adoption of the Buddhist and Hindu religions, the presence of the epics Mahabharata and Ramayana, and the use of the Sanskrit language, scripts and styles of temple architecture. Buddhism is still the dominant religion across the region from Myanmar to Vietnam, while Hinduism survives in pockets such as Bali. Despite the later impact of Islam, European colonial rule and postcolonial modernity, the influence of ancient Indian cultures remains alive in place and personal names, commonly used words, and in the arts and crafts.

There are some cultural artefacts that seem to have survived with little change from the very earliest phase of contact between the two regions. Traditional masks from Bali, Sri Lanka and the Andhra–Odisha coast are strikingly similar. The same is true of Wayang Kulit, the Indonesian art of shadow puppetry, and its equivalent in Odisha and Andhra Pradesh. It is fun to imagine ancient mariners entertaining each other through the long nights of an ocean crossing by enacting shadow puppet plays on their ship's sails as they made a perilous journey to distant lands.

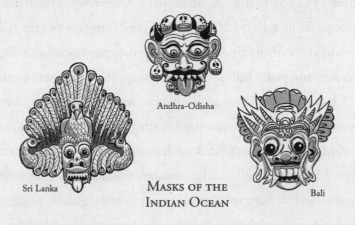

Andhra-Odisha

Sri Lanka

MASKS OF THE INDIAN OCEAN

Bali

Influences from the east made their way back home too. One commonplace example is the custom of chewing paan (betel leaves with areca nuts, usually with a bit of lime and other ingredients). While this is common across the Indian subcontinent, the areca nut (called supari in Hindi) is originally from South East Asia and was chewed across the region, even as far north as Taiwan.

Why Can't Everyone Just Get Along?

Most of the early known history of what are now the states of Kerala and Tamil Nadu is full of the rivalry between three clans—the Cholas, Cheras and Pandyas. The Cholas occupied the Kaveri delta, the Pandyas were near Madurai and the Cheras lived along the Kerala coast. Their fortunes waxed and waned over time, but it is amazing how the same three clans battled each other over fifteen centuries (from about 300 BC to AD 1200)! Early Tamil Sangam poetry tells a vivid story of the times featuring prosperous cities, bustling bazaars and ports full of merchant ships from foreign lands.

Excavations in Tamil Nadu in recent years have unearthed the remains of significant urban centres from this period such as one found under the hamlet of Keezhadi, near Madurai, in 2015. The findings confirm that the cities mentioned in Sangam literature are not imaginary. Sangam literature also celebrates the region's interactions with the rest of the world with descriptions of bustling ports and foreign trade. One of the texts also makes the first definite reference to a naval battle, in which the Chera king Udiyanjeral defeated an unnamed local enemy and took a number of Greek merchants captive (the captives were later freed after the king received a large ransom for them).

AD 300

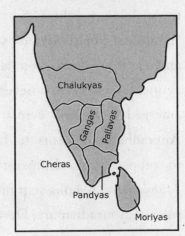

AD 600

AD 1000

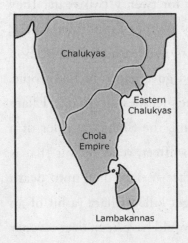

AD 1200

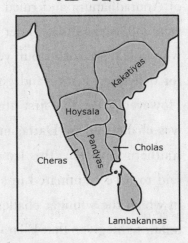

SOUTHERN KINGDOMS

By the fourth century BC, some Tamil groups began to settle in northern Sri Lanka. There was already a significant population of settlers from Odisha–Bengal, and the local Vedda population that had been sidelined, as mentioned earlier. Several small kingdoms gradually emerged, scattered across the island. One of these, Anuradhapura, seems to have gained prominence due to support from Emperor Ashoka. According to the *Mahavamsa*, Ashoka sent his son Mahinda to convert the ruler of Anuradhapura, Devanampiya Tissa, to Buddhism in the third century BC.

In 177 BC, two Tamil adventurers captured the throne of Anuradhapura and ruled it for twenty-two years. They were followed a decade later by another Tamil ruler, Ellara, who ruled for forty-four years and earned a reputation for delivering justice and good governance to his people. However, after the first three decades of peace, Ellara was challenged by Dattagamani, the Sinhalese ruler of a southern kingdom. This led to fifteen years of war that is said to have culminated in a face-to-face duel unto death in which the younger challenger killed Ellara (a bit of an unfair fight, given that Ellara would have been over seventy by this time!).

A modern conflict

Today, we think of relations between the Sinhalese and Tamils of Sri Lanka (and by extension between Buddhists and Hindus) as having been marked by perpetual conflict. In the second century BC, the Tamils and the Sinhalese would have seen themselves and each other as relatively recent immigrants. In fact, there seems to have been a long-term alliance between the Sinhalese and the Tamil Pandyas of Madurai against other Tamil clans like the Cholas.

After Dattagamani defeated Ellara and united the island, he established himself in Anuradhapura. Except for a couple of brief interruptions, the city would remain the capital of the island's dominant kingdom for the next thousand years. Just like the political history of the southern tip of India was mostly about the rivalries between three clans, this period of Lankan history would be dominated by the Moriya and Lamkanna clans. This was further complicated by intrigues within each clan.

The politics of the times is best illustrated by the story of Sigiriya, one of the most spectacular historical sites in Asia. Dhatusena, the king of Anuradhapura, was murdered by his son Kassapa in AD 477. Kassapa was the king's eldest son but

SIGIRIYA

by a junior concubine and consequently not in the line of succession. So, he captured power with the help of Migara, his cousin, who was the army commander. The crown prince Moggallana, however, escaped to southern India (probably finding shelter in the Pandya court). Kassapa then decided to build a new capital for himself at Sigiriya. It is a site dominated by a gigantic rock. The new capital was laid out at the foot of the rock while the palace was built on the top. The top is like a miniature Machu Picchu and provides amazing views of the surrounding countryside. Sigiriya's moment in the sun, however, came to an abrupt end in AD 495 when Moggallana suddenly returned with an army of Indian mercenaries. He defeated Kassapa and killed him, and shifted the capital back to Anuradhapura. Sigiriya was gradually abandoned except for parts that were used as a Buddhist monastery.

From Egypt to India

Even as maritime trade boomed in the eastern Indian Ocean, there was a similar boom in trade between India's west coast and the Greco-Roman world. The trade routes are described in detail in the *Periplus of the Erythraean Sea*, a manual written by an Egyptian–Greek merchant in the first century AD.

What's in a name?

The Erythraean Sea literally means Red Sea, but the term was used by the ancient Greeks more broadly to include the Indian Ocean.

The *Periplus* tells us that there were two routes from the Mediterranean to the Red Sea. One of the routes started from the ports of what are now Israel and Lebanon and made its way overland via Petra to the Gulf of Aqaba. The magnificent rock-cut remains of the city of Petra in Jordan, now a World Heritage Site, show us how the Nabataeans, the Arab people whose capital city it was, had grown rich from trade.

The alternative route for Roman merchants to the Red Sea ran through the cosmopolitan port city of Alexandria in Egypt. From Alexandria, there were two options. One could make one's way directly from the Nile delta to Suez. This was not a new route and we know from Herodotus that the ancient pharaohs had attempted to build a canal from the Nile to the Red Sea, and that the project had been completed during the rule of Persian emperor Darius in the sixth century BC. However, the canal kept getting silted up, and despite being re-excavated by the Ptolemies (the ruling dynasty of Egypt) in the third century BC, part of the journey had to be made on foot. At the time the *Periplus* was written, the more popular option was to sail up the Nile to Coptos (Qift) and then cross the desert for eleven days to arrive at the port of Berenice (Berenike) on Egypt's Red Sea coast.

From Berenice, the first port down the coast one could travel to was a 'fair-sized village' called Adulis. This was a barren stretch of the coast, but Adulis served as the nearest access to the city of Aksum that had emerged as a major urban centre in the Ethiopian highlands. We are told that Aksum was eight days' journey inland and was the source of ivory and rhino horn. At this stage, the Ethiopians had not yet converted to Christianity—one can still see gigantic stone obelisks in Aksum, probably carved in memory of the pagan kings of that period. The monarchs of Ethiopia were crowned in Aksum right upto the twentieth century. As the merchant fleets made their way further down the Red Sea, they would likely have passed the point at which the Arabian Peninsula comes nearest to the African coast (this may have been where our early ancestors exited Africa to travel all over the rest of the world!). The *Periplus* warns us that contrary winds and strong currents made this place dangerous for ships. The Arabs would later name it Bab-el-Mandeb or Gateway of Tears.

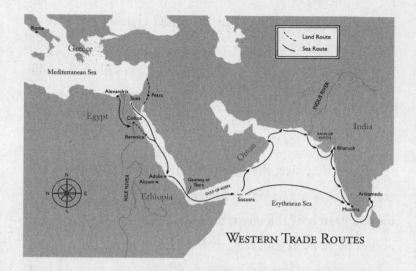

WESTERN TRADE ROUTES

After the narrow strait, the sea widens out to the Gulf of Aden. The *Periplus* tells us that this region was the source of frankincense. Merchants did not spend much time here as the place had a reputation for being unhealthy and 'pestilential even to those sailing along the coast'. Instead, they headed for the island of Socotra. Socotra is a fragment left over from the break-up of the supercontinent of Gondwana and its long isolation has left it with unique flora and fauna. One can still read graffiti left by these ancient mariners on the walls of the Hoq cave on the island.

The traditional coastal route to India from Socotra was to head north to Oman. This coast was controlled by the Persians at that time. Past the mouth of the Persian Gulf, the sailors would hit the Makran coast. From here, the ships would sail more directly eastwards towards the Indus delta. The *Periplus* reports that Sindh and parts of Gujarat were at this time controlled by the Sakas (Scythians) and Parthians. Beyond the Indus, the text says that there was a large gulf that ran inland but was too shallow to be navigable. This is the Rann of Kutch and one can see that, by the first century AD, it was no longer possible to sail across it as in Harappan times. Next along the coast was the town of Baraca (possibly Dwarka) after which the land gradually became more fertile and yielded a variety of crops—wheat, rice, sesame and, most importantly, cotton.

Having sailed past Saurashtra and the Gulf of Khambhat, the tired merchant ships would finally reach the estuary of the Narmada that led to the great port of Barygaza (Bharuch). The *Periplus* describes how shifting silt and sandbars made the entrance to the river perilous. Thus, the king of Barygaza appointed experienced fishermen as pilots to guide merchant ships. We are also warned of a wicked bore tide that could tear a ship from its moorings. The nautical details are so vivid that it is very likely that the author of the *Periplus* personally visited the place.

The most important exports from Barygaza were different kinds of cotton textiles, which are still exported from this region. Iron and steel products would have also been exported as we know that these were coveted by communities living along the Red Sea. In exchange, one of the most important products ancient Indians imported was wine—and we are told that Italian wine was preferred over the Arabian and Syrian stuff. The local kings also seem to have imported 'beautiful maidens for the harem'. With imported Italian wines and beautiful maidens, it is fair to say that the Sakas and the nobility of the Indian subcontinent of that period knew how to lead the high life.

The *Periplus* shows that the Romans were aware that from Barygaza, India's western coast ran south in almost a straight line. The text lists a number of ports down the coast but arguably the most important was Muzeris (or Mucheripatanam as the Indians called it), which was the source of black pepper. We are told of how Arab and Greek ships flocked to the port. Excavations at the village of Pattanam, just north of modern Kochi, have recently allowed archaeologists to exactly identify the location of this ancient port. Many kinds of imported artefacts have been found here, but some of the most common are wine and olive oil amphorae (terracotta storage jars) from as far away as France, Spain, Egypt and Turkey.

The reason that the port of Muzeris was experiencing a boom in international trade when the *Periplus* was written is that mariners had worked out in the previous century that they could use the monsoon winds to sail directly between

Socotra and southern India without hugging the coast. The author of the *Periplus* credits this discovery to a Greek pilot called Hippalus. It is curious that it took a Greek to work out how to harness the monsoon winds in the Arabian Sea when the Indians had been using them for generations in the Bay of Bengal to visit South East Asia. Perhaps ancient Arab and Indian mariners would have disputed Hippalus's claim. The *Periplus* mentions Greeks and Arabs in Muzeris but not Jews. However, a small Jewish trading community would have existed by the time the manual was written and, within a few decades, an influx of refugees would expand it significantly. After the Second Temple in Jerusalem was destroyed by the Romans in AD 70, many Jewish refugees came to settle around Muzeris. Thus, India became home to one of the oldest Jewish communities in the world.

Similarly, the Syrian Christian community claims descent from those converted by St Thomas, who is said to have visited these parts in the first century AD. Although the historical veracity of St Thomas' visit has been disputed by scholars, it is reasonably certain that Christians visited and settled along the Kerala coast a very long time ago. We know that a group of Christians fleeing persecution in the Persian Empire came to India under the leadership of Thomas of Cana in AD 345. Seventy-two families settled near Muzeris and were given special trading privileges by the local king. A few centuries later, early Muslims would build the Cheraman Masjid, said to be the world's second-oldest mosque, in the same general area. It is a testimony to the importance of ancient Muzeris that these early Jewish, Christian and Islamic sites are all located within a very short distance of each other.

From the *Periplus*, we can gather that the Romans knew that the coast south of Muzeris ended in a cape—Kanyakumari—and that the island of Taprobane (i.e., Sri Lanka) lay beyond it. Given the repeated mention of the Pandyas, but not of the rival clans, it seems that the *Periplus* was composed at a time when the Pandyas were dominant. We know from archaeological excavations that Roman traders made their way up the east coast as far as Arikamedu, close to modern Puducherry. The *Periplus* gets increasingly garbled as one goes further up the east coast. It shows an awareness of the Gangetic delta and mentions oriental tribes, but the details are quite blurred. The inland city of Thinae is mentioned as the source of silk. So, it is fair to say that this was the limit of what the Romans knew about the Indian Ocean in the first century AD.

Indo-Roman trade boomed in the first and second centuries AD. The Roman emperor Trajan had the Nile–Suez canal re-excavated; it began just south of modern Cairo and headed due east to the Red Sea. About 120 ships made the round trip between India and the Red Sea ports every year. The availability of eastern luxuries transformed Roman tastes, but the problem was that the empire ran a persistent trade deficit with India. This deficit had to be paid in gold and silver coins. Roman writer Pliny (AD 23–79) complained bitterly that 'not a year passed in which India did not take fifty million sesterces away from Rome'.

Other ancient globetrotters

Merchants were not the only people who travelled between the Roman Empire and India. We know, for instance, that it was fashionable for wealthy Roman women to consult Indian astrologers. We also have the story of Demetrius, a student of Greek philosophy, who was wrongly accused of stealing from a temple and arrested in Egypt. After he was exonerated and freed with compensation, he gifted all his property to a friend and sailed to India to study philosophy.

In a world where precious metals were used for minting coins, this was equivalent to severe monetary tightening. The Romans initially tried to solve the problem by curtailing trade, but eventually they would resort to debasing their coins (i.e., reducing the content of gold and silver in each coin). This would eventually cause distortions and inflation in the Roman Empire. Interestingly, the Indians continued to accept the debased coins although they recognized the higher quality of the older, high-content coins, which continued to circulate in the Indian Ocean long after the reigns of emperors who had issued them.

Stitched Ships

One of the most common observations made by ancient and medieval travellers is that ships on the Indian Ocean had hulls that were 'stitched' together with rope rather than nailed around a frame. This design most likely originated in India but seems to have been adopted by the Yemeni and Omani Arabs at an early stage. It is unclear why the Indians preferred to stitch together their ships when they were more than familiar with iron nails and had the technology for rust-resistant iron.

One possibility is that the stitched technique gave the hull a degree of flexibility. This meant that the ship was less likely to break if it ran into an obstruction like a shoal or sandbar. This was no small concern given that the Indian coastline had few natural harbours and most of the ports were either in an estuary or required sailing through a narrow passage, like that of Lake Chilika. Moreover, using the monsoon winds implied that the sailing season coincided with rough surf. This meant that arriving ships were often beached rather than tied by the quayside.

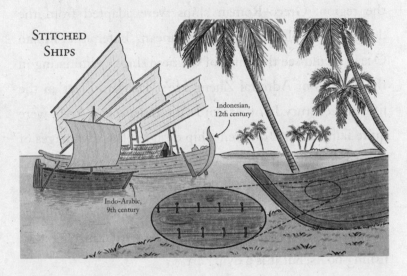

STITCHED SHIPS

Indonesian, 12th century

Indo-Arabic, 9th century

The Indo-Arab stitched ships, however, were not the only ones plying the Indian Ocean. The South East Asians had their own design derived from the outrigger canoes that their prehistoric ancestors had used. Perhaps the best depiction of eighth-century Indonesian outrigger ships is carved on the panels of Borobudur, Java. Using the panels as their guide, a group of enthusiasts recently recreated the 'Borobudur Ship'. Between August 2003 and February 2004, they further proved their point by sailing the reconstructed ship, named *Samudra Raksha*, from Java to Madagascar and then all the way to Ghana. The ship is now displayed at a museum in Borobudur.

In addition to the local ship designs, the Indian Ocean also witnessed maritime technologies derived from outside the region. Greco-Roman ships were adapted from the designs that plied the Mediterranean. Later, the Indian Ocean would see the entry of Chinese ships, culminating in the voyages of Admiral Zheng He's 'Treasure Fleet' in the fifteenth century. In other words, the Indians and Arabs were quite familiar with different ship designs. The advantages of the stitched design must have been significant if it remained the preferred technique till the Europeans arrived at the end of the fifteenth century. There are still a few coastal villages in India that have preserved the skill of stitching together fishing boats, but it is a dying art.

The Making of Madagascar

Madagascar is located close to Africa but, as you might remember from Chapter 1, the two land masses separated about 160 million years ago when Gondwana split up. Thus, the island's flora and fauna evolved in isolation and bore little resemblance to that of nearby Africa. For instance, it was home to the elephant bird that stood three metres tall and weighed half a ton, the largest bird ever. Then there was the giant lemur that was larger than a gorilla and was the world's largest primate.

As knowledge of the winds and sea currents improved, seafarers became confident enough to cross the ocean directly. One of the most intriguing examples of this is the colonization of Madagascar by the Indonesians. At some point in the fifth century, Indonesian sailors in their outrigger boats began to visit the island. Recent genetic studies show that the first permanent settlement of the island was of a tiny group from Indonesia around AD 800. Also, Malagasy, the island's main language, has been traced back to south Borneo.

Predictably, humans were a shock to the isolated and fragile ecosystem of the island. The extinction of the elephant bird and the giant lemur coincided with the arrival of people and it is difficult to escape the conclusion that these events are somehow related. We saw how the arrival of humans in Australia had a very similar impact. The settlers would come to be known as the Waqwaq, probably after their 'waqa' canoes. They were considered pirates by medieval Arab merchants sailing down the East African coast and generated fear among them. The Waqwaq also made regular raids on the mainland to acquire slaves. We have records of how they even made an unsuccessful attempt to capture the fortified port of Qanbalu, on the island of Pemba (in present-day Tanzania) in AD 945. However, coastal Madagascar eventually came to be dominated by the Arabs and Africans.

Many of the Waqwaq then withdrew to the island's central highlands where they slowly forgot their seafaring days.

The Bantu Migrations

Even as the Indian Ocean world witnessed an increase in maritime trade, the interiors of sub-Saharan Africa were experiencing profound demographic changes. Today, sub-Saharan Africa is dominated by Bantu-speaking people, but this was not always the case. Linguistic and, more recently, genetic data confirm that the Bantu people originated in what is now Nigeria and Cameroon around 5000 years ago, that is, the third millennium BC.

Around the first millennium BC, they began to expand out of their original homeland. Roughly speaking, one branch pushed directly south into equatorial Central Africa, through what is now the Democratic Republic of Congo. Another branch pushed east towards the East African Rift Valley before migrating south through what is now Kenya, Tanzania, Malawi and Zimbabwe. As they pushed into these new areas, the Bantu replaced or assimilated with the people who already lived there. Until their arrival, hunter-gatherers related to the Khoi-San had inhabited eastern and southern Africa, while Central Africa had been inhabited by the Pygmies. The Bantu, however, steadily replaced both groups.

The success of the Bantu seems to have been driven initially by their skills at farming but from around 600 BC, it was strengthened by locally developed iron technology. In Gabon, for instance, archaeological evidence shows iron-using farmers replacing stone-tool users around 300 BC. The process of migration still took many centuries and had not yet penetrated the southern tip of Africa when the Europeans arrived there. Thus, when Bartholomew Diaz and Vasco da Gama arrived at the Cape of Good Hope at the end of the fifteenth century, they encountered Khoi-San pastoralists and hunter-gatherers. It is estimated that the Khoi-San population at that time was around 50,000 in the south-western Cape. However, they would steadily lose territory to the Bantu tribes and to the Europeans.

CHAPTER 5

PEOPLE ON THE MOVE

The trade routes of the Indian Ocean became even more firmly established in the fourth and fifth centuries AD. It was around this time that the empire of the dynasty called the Guptas was established. Originating in the eastern Gangetic plains (in what is now Bihar and eastern Uttar Pradesh), the dynasty's first emperor was Chandragupta, but it was his son Samudragupta (AD 336–370) who dramatically expanded the empire. In a series of military campaigns, he established direct or indirect control over large parts of India. The empire was expanded further by Samudragupta's son Chandragupta II (also called Vikramaditya), who reigned between AD 375 and 413.

The Guptas, who were Hindus, generally followed a policy of religious tolerance, and records show that they gave permission for Buddhist monasteries and universities to be established during their reign. Also, with peace established over such a large territory, the Gupta era witnessed extraordinary economic and cultural prosperity. The empire's ports in Gujarat and Bengal were full of merchants, diplomats, scholars and pilgrims from China, Persia, Arabia, Ethiopia and the eastern Roman Empire.

Sailing Home with Fa Xian

A Chinese scholar called Fa Xian (also spelt Fa Hien) came to India in the fifth century by land, via Central Asia. He spent several years in northern India studying Buddhist texts. Fa Xian leaves us with the impression that India was a prosperous and well-governed empire under the Guptas.

Most interestingly, he also left us a vivid account of his return journey by sea. Around AD 410, Fa Xian left the Gupta capital of Pataliputra and made his way down the Ganga. There were several ports in Bengal during this period. One of these ports was Chandraketugarh, the remains of which have been uncovered thirty kilometres north of modern-day Kolkata. Archaeologists excavating a mound near Kolkata airport have recently found the remains of another ancient settlement. Fa Xian would have sailed past all these settlements as he made his way to the most important port in Bengal—Tamralipti. The site of this famous port of antiquity is now called Tamluk, a couple of hours south-west of Kolkata.

Fa Xian remained in Tamralipti for two years copying sacred documents. He then boarded a big merchant ship that set sail with the first winds of the winter monsoons. It took fourteen days for the ship to reach Sri Lanka. Fa Xian spent another two years on the island, studying and copying various scriptures. Next, Fa Xian set sail for South East Asia on board a large merchant vessel. The ship must have been fairly large as it carried 200 people and had a smaller vessel accompanying it with stores. Unfortunately, after two days of fair weather, the ships ran into a major storm and the larger ship sprang a leak. In a panic, some of the passengers tried to forcibly board the smaller ship. The crew of the smaller ship, fearing a stampede, cut the towing cable and sailed away. With little choice, the merchants began to throw their valuable cargo overboard to save their ship (Fa Xian threw away his water basin and pitcher). He feared he would be forced to throw away his beloved books too, but the weather cleared up.

After thirteen days, the ship was beached at a small island, and the leak was repaired. No one was sure about the location of the island and there were fears that they would be attacked by pirates (it is likely that this was one of the islands off the north Sumatra coast or perhaps one of the Nicobar Islands). Eventually, the crew got its bearings and set a new course. After ninety days at sea, they finally reached Java. Fa Xian spent five months there.

FA XIAN'S SHIP,
5TH CENTURY
(Recreation)

Then, he boarded a merchant ship headed for China. The crew alone numbered 200 men, indicating that this must have been a rather large vessel. We are told, furthermore, that the ship carried adequate provisions for fifty days. Fa Xian was very comfortable on this ship and it is possible he even had a cabin. After a month at sea, however, they were hit by a major storm, which had the ship veering off course. They could not sight land even after seventy days at sea; provisions and water began to run desperately low and the crew members started blaming each other. Fed up with the bickering, some of the more experienced merchants took charge and set a new course to the north-west. Eventually, after another twelve days, they arrived on the Chinese coast.

This narrative is fascinating at many levels. It provides the earliest first-hand description of an actual voyage in the eastern Indian Ocean. It also tells us that by the fifth century, there was a well-established sea route from Bengal to Sri Lanka and onwards to China via South East Asia. Despite all the dangers, there were large ships and experienced merchants that seem to have routinely made the journey.

The Sign of the Serpent

As you read in the previous chapter, the early history of the southern tip of India is dominated by the three clans—the Cheras, Pandyas and Cholas, with the Sinhalese kings of Sri Lanka sometimes entering the fray, usually as allies of the Pandyas. A few other dynasties did insert themselves into the story for significant periods of time. Perhaps the most important of these were the Pallavas of Kanchipuram. A Pallava kingdom already existed when Samudragupta embarked on his southern campaign. However, there is a long-standing debate about the origins of this dynasty. The texts and inscriptions variously hint at a Chola prince, an Andhra chieftain or a Brahmin scholar, or even someone of Parthian origins. Nevertheless, all the available evidence agrees that the dynasty gained its royal status via marriage to a princess of the Naga clan. Perhaps this explains the especially close links between the Pallavas and the Indianized kingdoms of South East Asia.

The Naga connection

The term 'Naga' was often used to refer to people with oriental features in north-east India or in South East Asia (i.e., the Sundaland diaspora). The Pallavas are known to have had links with kingdoms in South East Asia that used the serpent as a symbol or called themselves the serpent people. It raises the possibility that the Naga princess who helped found the Pallava dynasty was from South East Asia—maybe a descendant of Princess Soma and Kaundinya!

In the sixth century AD, the Pallavas began to expand their kingdom under a king named Simha-Vishnu, who defeated the Cholas, the Pandyas and a mysterious tribe called the Kalabhras. Having secured themselves to the south, the Pallavas then turned their attention to the north, where they came in conflict with the Chalukyas who had carved out a large kingdom in the region of the present-day states of Karnataka and Maharashtra. Simha-Vishnu had a younger brother named Bhima who sailed to a distant land and became a ruler after marrying a local princess. Five generations later, when Simha-Vishnu's direct descendant,

Parameswara Varman II, died suddenly without an heir, the Pallavas would bring back a twelve-year-old descendant of Bhima to sit on the throne.

This boy would be crowned Nandi Varman Pallavamalla or Nandi Varman II, a ruler who would eventually claw back the kingdom and become one of the greatest monarchs in the history of southern India. Nandi Varman II would rule his kingdom until AD 796, presiding over an economic and cultural boom. We know about the remarkable tale of how a foreign prince was invited to rule over a kingdom in southern India because Nandi Varman II himself tells us the story in inscriptions and bas-relief panels on the walls of the Vaikuntha Perumal temple in Kanchipuram. It is interesting that his inscriptions emphasize that he was a 'pure' Pallava. One explanation would be that, being foreign-born, he needed to firmly emphasize his right to the throne. However, the oriental faces in the temple panels suggest he was not shy of his South East Asian links. Perhaps the term 'pure' has a somewhat different meaning. The Pallava dynasty began with a marriage to a Naga princess. So Nandi Varman II may have been making a different point—that he was the descendant of a Pallava prince—that is, Bhima—and a Naga queen and, consequently, a true Pallava.

At the height of their power, the Pallavas controlled Tamil Nadu, southern Karnataka, Andhra Pradesh and parts of Sri Lanka. Their capital of Kanchipuram and their main port in Mahabalipuram were impressive cities that the Pallava kings adorned with large Hindu temples. Several of them have survived in both locations and are well worth a visit.

PALLAVA LIGHTHOUSE, MAHABALIPURAM

Modern-day tourists visiting Mahabalipuram usually see the rock-cut caves and the Shore Temple, but do not often notice the remains of a Pallava-era lighthouse near the modern lighthouse that is on a hill behind the ancient monuments. The Pallava lighthouse was built around AD 630, and a fire was kept burning here every night in order to guide ships to the port.

A city submerged

Most of the Pallava-era port city at Mahabalipuram is now underwater. There is an old legend that there were originally seven temples on the shore. It was said that the city's wealthy citizens grew so arrogant that the gods sent a great flood to punish them. The flood swept away all but one of the temples, the lonely Shore Temple that we see today. Historians had long discounted this oral history despite claims by local fishermen that their nets routinely got entangled in stone structures in the sea. Then, in December 2004, a deadly tsunami hit coastlines across the Indian Ocean. Before the tsunami came in, the sea first withdrew and, for a few minutes, exposed several stone structures off the coast of Mahabalipuram. Later investigations by the Archaeological Survey of India confirmed that there are indeed several temples and man-made structures that lie submerged off the coast. Moreover, studies of the area have found evidence that this coastline has been hit by tsunamis repeatedly and it is possible that the flood mentioned in the legend relates to a tsunami.

By the eighth century, there were several well-developed kingdoms in South East Asia. The Srivijaya kingdom covered most of Sumatra and the Malay Peninsula. It had two major urban hubs—Palembang on Sumatra and Kadaram on the peninsula. Java was another major political centre. Its kingdoms steadily extended their influence over islands such as Bali and Madura until it later grew into the great Majapahit Empire that controlled a large swathe of what is now Indonesia. In Cambodia, the Khmers were welded into a kingdom that culminated in the Angkor Empire. Further east, the kingdom of Champa stretched along the central and southern coast of Vietnam (some historians argue that it was more a confederacy than a centralized kingdom). These kingdoms traded with each other and with India and China. They also fought bitter wars, particularly the Khmers versus the Chams, and the Javans versus Srivijaya.

Given the close political and commercial links between the Pallavas and these kingdoms, it is not surprising that the dominant source of Indian influence in South East Asia shifted from Odiya to Tamil during this period. For instance, the South East Asians adopted the Pallava version of the Brahmi script. This is why the scripts used to write Khmer, Thai, Lao, Burmese and Javanese-Kawi are derived from the Pallava script. Till the early nineteenth century, the Brahmi-derived Baybayin script was even used to write

Tagalog in the Philippines. And, as we saw from Fa Xian's account, the trade routes between India and China were well established by the fifth century. By the Pallava period, there were large Indian merchant communities living in Chinese ports.

Arabia Divided

It was also rivalries between clans—in this case, the Sabeans, Hadhramis and the Himyar—that shaped the history of ancient Yemen. From the second century AD, the dynamics of the region began to change due to demographic, cultural and geopolitical shifts. Initially, the region witnessed the arrival of a large Jewish trader and refugee community from the west. The descendants of these Jewish settlers would survive in both Ethiopia and Yemen until the twentieth century. Meanwhile, waves of Arabs from the area around modern Riyadh began to encroach into neighbouring territories. One branch pushed into Yemen and Oman. It is not clear why these large-scale migrations took place, but Arab names suddenly start to appear in Yemeni inscriptions. The records suggest growing Arab assertiveness against the local clans as their numbers grew.

In response to this, some Yemeni groups migrated north into Oman, which was witnessing its own Arab migration.

Over time, these two migrations displaced or absorbed the existing Persianized population in Oman. To this day, most Omanis can trace their ancestry to the two migrations; the Yamani clans claim Yemeni origin and the Nizari clans claim central Arabian origin. The Sabeans were, meanwhile, forced to accept an alliance with the Himyar who, for a while, imposed control over southern Arabia. However, the Himyar were themselves caught between the two great powers of the time—the Sassanian Empire of Persia and their bitter rivals, the Byzantines. By this time the Byzantines (that is, the eastern Roman Empire with its capital in Constantinople, modern Istanbul) had become enthusiastic Christians, and geopolitics took on a religious colour. The Byzantine emperor Constantius (337–361) dispatched ambassadors and a missionary named Theophilus the Indian to the Himyarite court to demand permission to build churches and proselytize.

One of the kingdoms profoundly impacted by this churn in geopolitics and religion was Aksum (in the north of modern-day Ethiopia). Around the middle of the fourth century AD, the Aksumites captured two Christian teenagers, Frumentius and Edesius, from a merchant ship on the Red Sea. They were taken to the capital city, Aksum, where they served as slaves of the king. They soon came to be trusted. Shortly before his death, the king granted them their freedom and promoted them to high office. The widowed queen became dependent on them for running the kingdom and also entrusted the education of her infant son, the new king, to Frumentius. The former slaves now used their position to actively promote Christianity, and eventually, under the influence of his tutor, the young king, Erazanes, also converted to the faith. This brought Aksum into the cultural and geopolitical sphere of influence of the Byzantines.

In the early sixth century, the Aksumite king Ella Asbeha attacked Yemen and placed a Christian king on the Himyar throne. Once the invaders withdrew, there was a revolt against the Christians led by the Jews and the pro-Persian faction, and the country plunged into a bloody civil war. A Jewish warlord called Yusuf captured the throne and attacked the chain of fortifications around the Straits of Bab-el-Mandeb. Contemporaneous accounts tell us that the raid left 12,500 dead and 11,000 captives (and yielded 2,90,000 sheep, oxen and camels as spoils of war). Ella Asbeha was not long in responding. He assembled a large army and a fleet to attack Yemen. Yusuf and his allies were killed and a Christian king was again put on the throne. The Aksumites also left behind a garrison and stipulated that the Yemeni had to pay a tribute to Aksum every year. However, soon after Ella Asbeha left, the garrison went rogue and replaced the king with their own candidate. In this way, a complicated civil war laid waste a prosperous land.

Eventually some order was restored by the part-legendary hero Sayf ibn Dhi-Yazan who used Persian help to evict the Aksumites. Sayf became king under the understanding that he would pay tribute to the Sassanian monarch. However, Sayf was stabbed to death by a group of Ethiopian slaves and the Persian army was dispatched once again. This time the region was put under direct Persian rule. These events need to be seen in the broader context of the prolonged wars between the Persians and Byzantines across the Middle East. The campaigns in Yemen were part of an attempt by the Byzantine–Ethiopian alliance to take control of the Red Sea trade route to India and bypass the rival Persian Gulf route. As a contemporary Byzantine put it, 'For it was impossible for the Ethiopians to buy silks from the Indians, since the Persian merchants always locate themselves in the very harbours where the Indians first put in, as they inhabit the adjoining country and are accustomed to buy the whole cargo.'

As if the wars were not enough, the Middle East was also devastated by a deadly pandemic. Known as the Plague of Justinian, it was first reported in Egypt around AD 541. Egyptian grain ships then took it to the Byzantine capital Constantinople, where it is said to have killed half the population. It soon spread across the Mediterranean and the Middle East where, over a few decades, it killed an estimated 25–50 million people. Thus, when the seventh century dawned, the Middle East was exhausted. These were the circumstances in which a completely new force emerged—Islam.

The Rise of an Empire

The sudden rise of Islam radically changed the power dynamics of the western Indian Ocean in the seventh century. As is well known, Prophet Muhammad was initially not successful in convincing his own tribe, the Quraysh of Mecca, of his message. In AD 622, he and his followers slipped away to Medina. Their fortunes began to turn after they successfully defended Medina against an alliance of their enemies in AD 627. This battle is now remembered as the Battle of the Trench as Muhammad used trenches to neutralize the enemy's superior cavalry. Within three years, he captured Mecca and carved out a significant kingdom in the Arabian Peninsula.

Having secured his base, the Prophet sent out messengers to the chieftains of neighbouring tribes asking them to join his cause. This included Yemeni and Omani groups that had tired of Persian rule and wanted to push them out. Muhammad's envoy is said to have arrived just as the Omanis, led by King Julanda, were contemplating a major offensive against the Persians. The Persians held the coast while the Omanis held the mountains in the interior. The Julanda princes received the envoy in Nizwa, an oasis surrounded by tall craggy mountains. The message offered support to them if they accepted Islam and threatened armed conflict if they did not. In response, the Omanis did accept Islam, and in fact were among the first to convert to the religion. Fortified by the new faith and the promise of Muhammad's support, the Omanis proceeded to oust the Persians from the settlements along the coast.

The Prophet died in AD 632, just two years after he had conquered Mecca. However, his immediate successors rapidly expanded the territory they controlled. The Arabs defeated the Persians at the Battle of Qadisiyyah in AD 637 which led to the fall of Ctesiphon, the capital of the Sassanians. Soon, they took over the whole of the Persian Empire. The Byzantines put up a more spirited resistance in their heartlands of Anatolia, but the Arabs captured Jerusalem by AD 638 and controlled the whole of Syria, Palestine and Egypt by AD 641. Yemeni and Omani warriors played an important role in these early conquests.

Within a decade of Muhammad's death, the Arabs came to control a vast empire. Unfortunately, such a rapid increase in wealth and power inevitably led to rivalries and tensions within the newly emerging elite. The power struggle culminated in the Battle of Karbala in AD 680 where Muhammad's grandson Husain ibn Ali and his followers were massacred by a much larger army sent by Umayyad Caliph Yazid. Husain is said to have died with his infant son in his arms. This incident created the Shia–Sunni sectarian divide that exists to this day. Intriguingly, there is an oral tradition in India that Husain's party included a group of Hindu mercenaries who were also killed in the battle. This is why the Mohyal Brahmins of Punjab still join Shia Muslims in the annual ritual mourning of Muharram.

The Umayyads next decided to impose direct control over the Omanis who, as early and willing converts to Islam, had come to expect a degree of autonomy. Two brothers, Sulaiman and Said, organized a heroic defence against a large army of 40,000 sent by land and sea. The Omanis were initially successful, but the enemy kept getting reinforcements and eventually their resistance broke down. Around AD 700, the two brothers fled by ship with their families and followers to Africa. Thus began Oman's long relationship with the eastern seaboard of Africa, which the Arabs called the Land of Zunj.

Umayyad rule came to a bloody end in AD 750 when the dynasty was violently overthrown by Abu-al-Abbas, after which a wave of refugees fled to Africa. In this way, the east coast of Africa came to have a smattering of Arab settlements. Meanwhile, the remaining Omanis withdrew once more to the rough Al Hajar mountains around Nizwa. There they developed a distinct branch of Islam called Ibadhi. To this day, the majority of Omanis follow Ibadhi Islam.

Herodotus Again, and Sindbad the Sailor

Despite the disruptions caused by wars, merchants continued to sail between India and the Middle East. The initial years of the Abbasid caliphate were very bloody and rivals were mercilessly eliminated. Eventually, the Abbasids managed to establish order over the vast empire. They also shifted the capital from Damascus to Baghdad. Under the rule of Harun al-Rashid (AD 786–809), the empire enjoyed a period of peace and prosperity. However, at the same time, the relative simplicity of early Islam was replaced by a glittering court and the elaborate pomp reminiscent of the Sassanians. It was also a time when trade boomed in the western Indian Ocean.

The spirit of the times is echoed in the tales of *The Arabian Nights*. In the tale 'How Abu Hasan Broke Wind', we are told of a wealthy Yemeni merchant who had become very rich by trading with India. Having loudly farted at his own wedding, he fled social embarrassment by sailing off to India where he settled in the port of Calicut (or Kozhikode) in Kerala. We are informed that the local king, a Hindu, welcomed Arabs and that the port had a large community of Hadramawt Yemeni merchants. This is a vivid description of medieval globalization! In fact, Arab merchants in Kerala often took on local wives. Their descendants, the 'Mappila' Muslims, are now a quarter of Kerala's population—interestingly, the word 'mappila' means 'son-in-law' in Malayalam.

The Arabian Nights contains many tales about merchants and voyages but arguably the most entertaining are those of Sindbad. The collection contains several of his voyages, but his second voyage is especially interesting. It tells us that Sindbad's ship drops anchor near a beautiful island and he decides to go for a walk. Finding a nice spot, Sindbad falls asleep under a tree. Unfortunately, he sleeps for much longer than expected and, when he wakes up, he discovers that his ship has left without him! Alarmed at being abandoned on what seems to him an uninhabited island, he attempts to find a way to get out. The interesting part of the story for our purposes occurs when Sindbad finds himself trapped in a valley with very steep sides. He is surprised to find that the valley floor is covered in priceless diamonds. However, he also discovers that there are huge serpents sleeping in nearby caves and is afraid they will devour him as soon as they come out after sundown.

While thinking of ways to escape, a large chunk of meat lands near Sindbad and a giant eagle picks it up and flies off. Looking up, he sees that some people at the top of the ravine are throwing down large chunks of meat in the hope that some of the diamonds will stick to the flesh. When the eagles picked up the meat and took them to their nests, the people would scare the birds off by making a lot of noise and collect the diamonds. Sindbad sees his opportunity and fills his pockets with diamonds before tying himself to a piece of meat.

SINDBAD THE SAILOR

In due course, he is picked up by an eagle and thus escapes from the valley. The diamonds make him a rich man. Many readers will be familiar with this Sindbad adventure. What is remarkable is that a very similar tale was told by Herodotus when he wrote about how the Arabs acquired cinnamon. In other words, versions of this story had been circulating in the Indian Ocean region for over a thousand years!

The Conquest of Sindh

By AD 711, Arab armies had reached Spain and, within a few years, they won control of the Iberian peninsula. The Umayyads simultaneously pushed east and, in AD 705, an Arab army invaded the Makran coast and took over Baluchistan. This brought them to the borders of Sindh and the first direct encounter with Indic civilization. The kingdom of Sindh was ruled at that time by Raja Dahir, who was considered, according to the sources, an able and popular ruler. An initial exploratory expedition was repulsed, but in AD 711, a more substantial military force was sent out from Iraq under the leadership of a young general called Muhammad bin Qasim. The campaign is mainly recounted in a text called the *Chachnama*, which is also the basis for a history written some centuries later by the Mughal historian

Ferishta. According to Ferishta, the army first attacked Deval, a port in the Indus estuary, not far from modern Karachi. It seems that the town also had a large Hindu temple and was a place of pilgrimage. The town was defended by a fort garrisoned by 4000 Rajput soldiers. Muhammad bin Qasim directed a constant bombardment against the fort using catapults. Eventually the fort was stormed, and all the defenders massacred.

After receiving reinforcements from Iraq, the Arabs moved north to meet Dahir's main army. Muhammad bin Qasim used a barrage of burning naphtha balls to disrupt the enemy's elephants before making a cavalry charge. Although surrounded and severely wounded, Raja Dahir fought till he was killed on the battlefield. The Sindhis now withdrew to the fort of Ajdur under the command of their queen where they remained under siege for several months. Facing starvation, the queen and the survivors are believed to have emerged for a final charge and were massacred.

Despite the relative ease with which they had taken over Sindh, the Arabs did not expand beyond their foothold in the subcontinent. The Gurjara-Pratihara Empire ruled over much of north India at that time and its armies easily fended off the Arabs. Indian inscriptions also record that the Arabs attempted to push into the Deccan through Gujarat and were repulsed by the Chalukya king, Vikramaditya II.

Indic rulers seem to have made counter-raids and continued to rule over Afghanistan till the end of the tenth century.

With eastward expansion blocked off, the Arabs turned their attention north towards Central Asia. The Turkic people of the region mostly worshipped the sky god Tengri or were Buddhist. There were also Hindu and Zoroastrian influences. In the middle of the eighth century, they found themselves caught between two great powers. The Chinese Tang dynasty was pushing in from the east while the Abbasid caliphate was pushing in from its base in Iran. The two faced each other at the Battle of Talas in AD 751 in which the Arabs decisively defeated the Tang army. Thus, Central Asia came into the Islamic sphere of influence rather than the Chinese.

The Arrival of the Zoroastrians

When the Arabs conquered Persia in the seventh century, the majority of Iranians were Zoroastrian. After the conquest, however, more and more people converted to Islam. In the face of growing persecution, some of the remaining Zoroastrians fled to India. Their descendants survive to this day as the tiny Parsi community. One text that purports to recount this story is the *Qissa-i-Sanjan*, a text composed many hundreds of years later, around AD 1600. The text tells us that in the early tenth century, a small group of Zoroastrians left their homes in Khorasan, north-eastern Iran, and set out to look for a country where they could practise their religion in peace. They made their way south to the port of Hormuz from where these families sailed for India. It appears that they first landed on the island of Diu and spent a few years there. However, they still felt insecure and decided to head for a small Hindu kingdom on the Gujarati mainland around AD 936. The text says that the ruler of the kingdom was Jadi Rana (probably of the Jadeja Rajput clan) and describes him as 'liberal, sagacious and wise'.

The roaming Roma

Even as Arabs, Parsis and Jews were settling in India, at least one group of Indians migrated to the Middle East. Genetic studies have confirmed that the Roma, a European ethnic group, are the descendants of medieval migrants from north-western India. What were they doing in the Middle East? Given the long history of Indian soldiers in the region, it is possible that the ancestors of the Roma were mercenaries. A more intriguing possibility is that they were imported as metal workers. India was famous in the ancient and medieval world for its metallurgy and we know that the famous 'Damascus sword' used by Muslim armies in the Crusades was made with Indian steel technology. One thing is certain: they were not there as slaves because they would not have been allowed to stay as a cohesive group and maintain their culture.

Jadi Rana received the refugees warmly and listened patiently to their request for a place to settle. While he was sympathetic to their predicament, he was hesitant to let so many foreigners settle in his lands. There is a well-known legend, probably apocryphal, that the king asked one of his servants to bring a bowl filled with milk to the top. The message being that the bowl would overflow if any more milk was added. The leader of the Parsis, however, responded by adding some sugar to the milk. The dissolved sugar sweetened the milk but did not cause it to overflow. Thus, the account goes, the Parsis convinced the king. The *Qissa* contains a somewhat different version, in which Jadi Rana asked the Parsis to explain their religion and rituals to him. The king decided to give the Parsis refuge provided they accepted the following conditions in perpetuity: that they would give up arms; that they would adopt Gujarati as their language; that their women would wear local clothing; and finally, that all marriage ceremonies would be held in the evening. The refugees accepted the conditions and the Parsis came to settle in Gujarat.

CHAPTER 6

DYNASTIES, INVASIONS AND SHIPWRECKS

Even as the Arab conquests changed the political and cultural landscape of the western Indian Ocean, not much changed in the east: the Palas of Bengal and the Pallavas of Kanchi continued to trade with the Hindu–Buddhist kingdoms of South East Asia and beyond. Dynasties rose, empires expanded their borders and trade and military alliances were formed between kingdoms separated by the vast ocean; it is to this interconnected world that we now turn.

Who Built Angkor Wat?

In the second half of the eighth century, records tell us, the Khmers began to face raids from the kingdoms of Java. Not to be left out of the action, the Srivijaya king of Sumatra–Malaya also made a surprise raid on the hapless Khmers and killed the ruler of one of their kingdoms. Amidst this turmoil, a new ruler, Jayavarman II, came to the Khmer throne. It was he who founded the Angkor Empire, though not the city by which the empire is now known.

Very little is known about the origins of Jayavarman II but later inscriptions say that he came from Java to take the crown. Perhaps he was a Khmer prince taken away by the Javanese as a hostage, or, more likely, his claim to the Khmer throne was acquired by marriage to a Khmer princess. Once he came to power, he systematically subdued local rivals and fended off raiders from both Java and Srivijaya. A new capital called Indrapura was founded; it was the first of several new cities that Jayavarman II would establish. At the same time, the territories around the great lake of Tonle Sap were added to the growing kingdom and systematically settled.

Jayavarman II died sometime around or before AD 850. He was succeeded by his son, who seems to have consolidated the fledgling empire till AD 877. The king after him, Indravarman I, however, was the nephew of Jayavarman II's queen. Inscriptions also tell us that Indravarman I's wife traced her lineage back to the royal family of ancient Funan, the kingdom said to have been established by Kaundinya and the Naga princess; matrilineal descent seems to have been an important component of royal legitimacy in Angkor. It was under Indravarman I that the Khmers began to build the complex hydraulic network of canals and lakes that allowed a major expansion in rice cultivation. By the time his son and successor Yashovarman I wore the crown, the Khmers ruled much of what is now Cambodia, Thailand and Laos.

The empire now needed a grand capital and Yashovarman I laid out the first city in Angkor and named it Yashodharapura after himself. He also built a number of large Hindu temples. This includes the Preah Vihear temple, a UNESCO World Heritage Site, built on a mountaintop on the Thai-Cambodian border. Angkor grew and prospered through most of the tenth century, but there appears to have been instability and civil war at the beginning of the eleventh century. Yet again, power was captured by an outsider with a matrilineal claim to the throne. Suryavarman I was a prince of a vassal state, but his mother came from the same maternal line as that of Jayavarman II's queen and Indravarman I's mother's family.

Suryavarman I ruled over the empire for almost half a century (AD 1002–1050). He re-established control over territories that had broken away during the civil war and established temporary peace along the eastern border with Champa in southern Vietnam. He also expanded the capital and built a large palace complex that included a tiered pyramid called the Phimeanakas or Sky Palace. A modern-day visitor will almost certainly be told of the legend of how the ruling monarch was expected to spend the first watch of every night in the pyramid tower with a serpent princess in the form of a beautiful woman. While the bit about snakes turning into women seems implausible, the legend is a reminder of the importance of the Naga lineage in establishing the legitimacy of royal power. This is why the royal symbol of the Khmer kings was the seven-headed cobra, which shows up frequently in their art.

ANGKOR WAT

After Suryavarman I's death, the empire again suffered internal wars as well as renewed hostilities with Champa. In 1113, order was restored by another powerful leader, Suryavarman II. It was he who built Angkor Wat, still the largest religious building in the world and a UNESCO World Heritage Site. Its sheer scale must be seen to be believed but, in order to imagine what it looked like in its heyday, one must remember that the towers were originally covered in gold leaf. Angkor Wat was originally a temple dedicated to the Hindu god Vishnu. When it was adapted to Buddhist use in later times, the main idol of Vishnu was moved out of the sanctum to a corridor near the main entrance. Visitors will find that it is still lovingly worshipped by the locals.

After a period of stability under Suryavarman II, the familiar pattern of war and disorder repeated itself. Suryavarman II's successors were particularly harassed by repeated raids from Champa. In 1177, the Chams made a naval attack that bypassed the usual land defences and took the Khmers completely by surprise. The invaders managed to reach the capital, where the wooden palisades and moats of Yashodharapura proved inadequate. The Khmer king was killed and the city sacked. The empire descended into chaos. Once more, an energetic new leader, Jayavarman VII, came to the rescue of the empire. The maternal line was again important as he derived his legitimacy from the fact that his mother was Suryavarman I's granddaughter. The new king first dealt with the Chams and defeated them in a major naval battle that is vividly depicted on the wall of the Bayon temple. He then rebuilt the capital. Recognizing the limitations of the old defences, he built Angkor Thom to be more compact than Yashodharapura, but added laterite walls and a wide moat. Five stone causeways gave access to this royal city through monumental gates that were surmounted by gigantic human faces; this is the stuff of a million tourist photographs.

What was Angkor like as a living city?

In 1296, Chinese diplomat Zhou Daguan visited Angkor and stayed there for eleven months. He left a detailed account of his visit, which makes for fascinating reading. For instance, he wrote a vivid description of a royal procession. The processions were led by a body of cavalry accompanied by standards and music. A few hundred beautifully attired palace women followed, some carrying gold and silver vessels, others burning tapers and still others were female warriors with swords and shields. Ministers and princes seated on elephants came next, carrying gold and silver parasols according to their rank. After this came the queens and other women of the royal family—on palanquins and chariots. Finally, the king himself entered on a large elephant surrounded by an escort of palace guards, also on elephants.

At its height in the eleventh and twelfth centuries, Angkor was the largest urban agglomeration in the world. Analysis of satellite images have confirmed that the royal capital was surrounded by a densely populated, semi-rural 'suburbia' where non-agricultural activities were mixed in with intensive farming sustained by a complex water management system. Estimates vary, but it is reasonable to say that more than a million people lived in Greater Angkor.

Marketplaces

Zhou Daguan included descriptions of more mundane everyday life. He tells us that the rich lived in houses with tiled roofs while the poor used thatch. The floors were covered in matting, but there were no tables, chairs and beds. People both sat and slept on the mats. Moreover, the climate was so hot and humid that people sometimes got up at night to bathe. Interestingly, commerce in the marketplace was mostly conducted by women. By paying rent to the local authority, they could set up a stall by displaying their goods on a mat laid out on the ground. Such scenes can still be seen across India and South East Asia. While women shopkeepers are not unusual, their dominance in the marketplace is particularly visible in the north-east Indian states of Meghalaya and Manipur.

The Chinese, the Cholas and the Kingdom of Srivijaya

The Cholas, as you will remember, were one of the three clans who dominated the southern tip of India in ancient times. During the period of Pallava rule, they had accepted the overlordship of Kanchi but still retained significant political clout. At the end of the ninth century, a Chola general called Aditya helped the Pallavas crush a revolt by the Pandyas, another ancient Tamil clan. As a reward, he seems to have been given a sizeable amount of territory, which he used to build up his military capability. In AD 873, he marched against his Pallava overlords, and the last Pallava king Aparajita (whose name ironically means 'he who cannot be defeated') was killed.

Over the next several decades, the Cholas steadily expanded their kingdom. They repeatedly defeated the combined armies of the Pandyas and their Sri Lankan allies. However, not all their military campaigns went well. When the Cholas attempted to expand northwards, they were beaten back by the Rashtrakutas who had replaced the Chalukyas in the Deccan plateau. In fact, the Rashtrakutas pushed back and occupied the old Pallava capital of Kanchi. It took several years for the Cholas to recover from the defeat, but they seemed to have regained their lost territory by the time Rajaraja Chola came to the throne in AD 985.

Mekong River

Ayutthaya
Bangkok
Angkor
Tonle Sap Lake
Oc Eo

My Son

Ho Chi Minh City

Bhujang Valley

Melaka Straits
Melaka

Singapore

Sumatra

Palembang

B o r n e o

Jakarta
Yogyakarta

Borobudur
J a v a
Bali

Bali Sunda Straits

INDIAN OCEAN

Sri Vijaya

Singasari

Khmer

Champa

The Indianized Empires of South East Asia

Before 13th Century Javanese Expansion

Rajaraja is widely regarded by Tamils as their greatest king. He defeated the combined armies of the Pandyas, the Sinhalese and the ruler of Kerala. This gave him control over ports on both the eastern and western coasts. Next, he decided to teach the Sri Lankans a lesson. A naval raid was made on the north of the island and the Sinhalese capital of Anuradhapura was sacked. The Maldives was also added to the empire. As thanksgiving for his victories, Rajaraja then built the enormous Brihadeswara temple dedicated to Shiva, which is now a UNESCO World Heritage Site.

Rajaraja's son Rajendra assumed the throne in 1014. He initially had to put down revolts by the old rival clans and consolidate his control over Sri Lanka. He then led an extraordinary military expedition that made its way north to the banks of the Ganga. Although the Cholas did not attempt to maintain control over these northern lands, Rajendra was clearly very proud of having made his way to the holy river. Water from the Ganga was carried back in golden vessels and a new capital was built—Gangaikonda Cholapuram, meaning 'The City of the Chola Who Brought the Ganga'.

From the perspective of Indian Ocean history, however, the most significant event of Rajendra's rule was a major naval raid on the Srivijaya kingdom of Sumatra and Malaya. The maritime trade route between India and China had by this time become very lucrative and there were two main routes. The first passed through the Straits of Malacca, between the Malay Peninsula and Sumatra. The Srivijaya kingdom controlled this route. The second, more southerly route, passed through the Sunda Straits between Sumatra and Java. Although it was a bit of a detour for those going to China or Champa, it had better access to the spice growing Maluku and Banda Islands. This route was usually controlled by the Javans. Not surprisingly, there was constant rivalry between the Srivijaya and the Javanese kingdoms.

The late tenth century was a period of prosperity in the Indian Ocean rim as trade boomed between the Song Empire in China, the Cholas in southern India and the Fatimid caliphate that controlled Egypt and the Red Sea. The rivalries of South East Asia were proving to be a major threat to this economic pipeline. In AD 987, a Srivijaya diplomatic mission made its way to China. During its stay in China, the diplomats were informed that their country was under attack from the Javan kingdom of Mataram. They decided to head home, but the war escalated and the mission found itself stranded in Champa for a year. It is likely that they received new instructions from the capital, for they headed back to China and pleaded with the Song emperor to place Srivijaya under its protection. Thus, China came to have influence in the region. The Srivijaya would have been aware that the entry of the Chinese into the Indian Ocean could elicit a response from the Cholas. Thus, they simultaneously sent missions to the Chola kings and made generous grants to Hindu and Buddhist temples in Chola ports!

The Srivijaya seem to have used Chinese protection to build up their own strength. Not surprisingly, this caused their neighbours to become concerned. Around 1012, Suryavarman I, the king of Angkor, chose to send an unusual gift to Rajendra Chola—his personal war chariot with which he had defeated his enemies. Such a gift would have had great symbolic importance and it is likely that Angkor was trying to woo the Cholas as a way to counterbalance the alliance between the Chinese and Srivijaya. It is also possible, that Angkor was trying to reopen the old trade route through the Isthmus of Kra as a way to bypass the contested straits. Meanwhile, in 1015, the Cholas themselves sent a direct diplomatic mission to China. But then, things suddenly changed in 1016 when the Srivijaya and their allies defeated the Javanese and sacked the capital of Mataram. This left Srivijaya in control of both sea routes. We have evidence to suggest that it soon exploited this situation by exacting exorbitant tolls on merchant ships. Rajendra Chola probably sent a small naval expedition to Sumatra in 1017 as a warning, but it was not taken seriously. Thus, the Chola returned in 1025 with a much larger fleet.

We do not know the exact sequence of events, but a study of the available information suggests the following: The fleet probably assembled near the main Chola port of Nagapattinam. Appropriately for a port that traded with South East Asia, the name means 'Port of the Nagas'. There is still a major port there, but the medieval port was probably several kilometres to the south. The Chola fleet would have first sailed south towards Sri Lanka before swinging east using ocean currents that would have taken them across to Sumatra. They probably then sailed down the west coast of the island towards the Strait of Sunda where they may have been resupplied by Javanese allies and picked up local guides. The fleet now made its way north into the Straits of Malacca and systematically sacked Srivijaya ports along the way. Finally, we are told that the Cholas decisively defeated the main Srivijaya army in Kadaram (now Kedah province in Malaysia). The invading force then withdrew, stopping at the Nicobar Islands on their way home.

The Chola raid significantly diminished Srivijaya power, but it is remarkable that the Chinese did not do anything to support Srivijaya. It is possible that the Chinese were just as annoyed at Srivijaya's rent extraction and had entered into an understanding with the Cholas. The Sumatrans too seem to have accepted their reduced status as they continued to send ambassadors to the Chola court and even participated in a joint diplomatic mission to China. Meanwhile, with external threats diminished, Java began to rebuild itself under a Balinese prince, Airlangga. The process of revival would culminate in the great Majapahit Empire in the fourteenth century.

Merchant Guilds and the Money Trail

During the Chola era, it is clear that maritime trade was an important part not only of the economies of kingdoms and empires but also in determining the relationships between these. So, how did medieval Indian merchants organize themselves? Were there individual merchants functioning under the umbrella of royal protection? Yes, individual merchants did exist and some of them were very wealthy and powerful. However, much of the trade was done by organizations called merchant guilds ('samaya' in inscriptions). One of the largest guilds, called the Five Hundred, was established in Aihole, Karnataka and it was something like today's multinational corporations. Another guild, called Manigramam, was formed in Tamil country and is even mentioned in Nandi Varman's inscriptions in Thailand!

Members of these guilds often came from a variety of backgrounds—for instance, the Five Hundred was founded by Karnataka Brahmins but would later be dominated by Tamil Chettiars. Moreover, guilds often worked with each other, with one guild giving another a contract to fulfil a certain need. Thus, the weavers' guild would contract with the merchants' guild to supply a certain amount of cloth for export. While the guilds often had links to the ruling dynasties, they were capable of making independent arrangements for themselves. This may be why business carried on irrespective of changing rulers and the wars they were engaged in. Some of the larger guilds even had companies of mercenaries—soldiers for hire—that protected their interests from attacks by pirates, rivals and even greedy rulers. In this way, the Manigramam guild survived several centuries till around AD 1300.

Interestingly, temples seem to have played an important part in financing the activities of the guilds. The early medieval period saw a sharp increase in temple building. It is well known that medieval temples were very wealthy, but the common impression is that this wealth was mostly granted to them by royals. In reality, the network of large and small temples had close links with merchant and artisan communities as well as village/town councils; this is quite clear from an examination of various donations and contracts. Moreover, the reason that the temples accumulated so much wealth is that they acted as bankers and financiers! For instance, a study of temple records has shown that temple lending was mostly directed to bodies like guilds and village councils rather than individual merchants. The temples lent money to village/town councils to build facilities, while they lent to merchant and artisan guilds for business. Thus, by the Chola period, Indian Ocean trade was no longer about individual merchants and small moneylenders, but involved a sophisticated network of guilds and those who financed them.

Sri Lanka, Then and Now

In the 1060s, the Chalukyas came to power once more in the region of Maharashtra and Karnataka, and took back their empire from the Rashtrakutas. As the revived Chalukyas expanded south, they came into conflict with the Cholas. Now, with the Cholas distracted by wars on their northern borders, the Sinhalese began to claw back their island under the leadership of Vijayabahu. Around 1070, the Cholas were finally pushed out. There may be a temptation to see the wars between the Cholas and the Sinhalese kings in terms of ethnic conflict. However, one must realize that the Sri Lankans were part of an anti-Chola alliance led by another Tamil clan, the Pandyas. Indeed, Vijayabahu's army had several Tamil mercenary units.

Having pushed the Cholas out, the Sinhalese would go on to help the Pandyas recover their kingdom on the mainland.

After Vijayabahu, the Sinhalese kingdom was consumed by civil war and broke up into several kingdoms. These were reunited by a king called Parakramabahu. Unfortunately, he had no sons and after his death Sri Lanka appears to have slid back into chaos. At this moment in history, a complete outsider managed to capture the throne. His name was Nissanka Malla, an Odiya prince, who used the Sinhalese link to ancient Kalinga to claim descent from King Vijaya (remember, the Kalingan prince who is said to have first settled the island in the sixth century BC). Given that his claim to the throne was always suspect, Nissanka converted to Buddhism and proclaimed that only a true Buddhist could be the king of Sri Lanka.

The Cholas watched all this and decided to back their own Odiya candidate—Magha of Kalinga. According to the *Culavamsa*, sequel to the *Mahavamsa*, Magha landed in Sri Lanka with 24,000 soldiers and proceeded to carve out a kingdom in the north of the island. Although the Cholas were no longer as strong as they once had been, they seem to have backed him as best they could. Magha also encouraged a lot of Tamils to settle in his kingdom.

As if things were not complicated enough, Sri Lanka suffered a naval invasion from South East Asia in 1247. It was led by Chandrabhanu, a prince from a kingdom on the Malay Peninsula. We do not know what prompted such a long-range expedition. It is possible that this was the last throw of the dice by the Cholas' allies in the Indian Ocean. The Sinhalese defeated the Malay prince with some difficulty and forced him to seek refuge in Magha's kingdom in the north. The prince from South East Asia then somehow managed to become the ruler of Magha's kingdom. So here we have an impossible combination of a Malay prince ruling over a Tamil kingdom founded by an Odiya adventurer in the north of Sri Lanka! It appears that Chandrabhanu still had ambitions of conquering the rest of the island and decided to make a second attempt. This time the Sinhalese asked for help from their traditional Pandya allies who defeated and killed Chandrabhanu. However, in exchange for their help, the Tamil clan took over the defeated king's territories. When the Pandyas later collapsed during the Muslim invasions, this territory would become an independent state.

This is the origin of the Tamil kingdom of Jaffna in northern Sri Lanka. It is quite extraordinary that two adventurers from faraway Odisha were at the heart of a rivalry that, in our own time, has come to be seen as Tamil–Sinhala conflict.

Inseparable Bonds of Friendship and Brotherhood

It should be clear by now that the Bay of Bengal and eastern Indian Ocean rim was an interconnected region, with links over vast distances established by maritime trade, cultural exchange, dynastic rivalries, marriage alliances and military operations. In the region of the western Indian Ocean rim and the Arabian Sea, it was a similar story.

The Yemeni port of Aden was a trade hub, and both Arab and Indian merchants flocked to it. During this period, the Jews established an elaborate business network that extended from the Mediterranean all the way to the west coast of India. Their detailed business records have survived through the centuries thanks to a lucky combination of dry climate and medieval superstition: they believed that they must not destroy any document with the name of God written on it. This included all business correspondence, so, when a merchant died, his papers were sent to a repository in Fustat, Old Cairo. This meant that tens of thousands of manuscripts have survived, and they provide a very vivid picture of the period.

For instance, take the letter from Mahruz, a Jewish merchant in Aden, to his cousin who had been attacked by pirates on the western coast of India. The cousin had then taken refuge in the Gujarati port of Bharuch (the same port mentioned a thousand years earlier in the *Periplus*). In the letter, Mahruz tells his cousin to get in touch with his Indian contact Tinbu for money and help, and touchingly mentions the 'inseparable bonds of friendship and brotherhood' between himself and the aforementioned Tinbu.

As we saw in the previous chapter, the east coast of Africa saw the establishment of a number of Arab and Persian settlements during the eighth and ninth centuries. Many of the settlers were from dissident (those who opposed the dominant group) Islamic sects—Ibadhi, Shia and Kharajite—who were fleeing persecution. They created a string of ports down the coast—Mogadishu, Mombasa, Kilwa, Zanzibar and so on. The migrants soon married local women and absorbed local influences. The Swahili language is the outcome of the interaction between Arabic and Bantu languages. Over time, the coastal settlements grew from refugee outposts into prosperous ports. The key to their prosperity was their role in supplying two commodities from the African hinterlands: slaves and gold. So many African slaves would be transported to the Middle East during this time that a revolt by them in AD 869 would result in them taking over much of southern Iraq, the heart of the Abbasid Empire. Known as the Zunj revolt, the rebels briefly ran an independent state that included the port of Basra. It would take the Abbasids fifteen years of armed conflict, bribery and amnesties to quell the rebellion. Despite this shock, slavery remained alive in the Middle East until as recently as 1962, when Saudi Arabia became the last country to abolish the practice.

Meanwhile, the interiors of Africa began to witness political and economic changes due to the demand for the evergrowing numbers of slaves and quantities of gold to the coast. By this time, the Bantu migrants had largely replaced or absorbed the ancient Khoi-San hunter-gatherers. Since the 1930s, archaeologists have uncovered evidence of the small kingdom of Mapungubwe that existed in the eleventh and twelfth centuries in the Limpopo valley in Zimbabwe. They have found beads from India and Egypt, which shows that goods from the Indian Ocean rim made it inland. The sites have also yielded the skeletons of a 'king' and a 'queen' who were buried along with gold ornaments and burial goods. Mapungubwe was soon superseded by a larger kingdom further north that has left behind the remains of hundreds of structures built in stone. The largest and most impressive of these structures are found in Great Zimbabwe, the kingdom's capital. The term *dzimba dzimabwe* means 'houses of stone' in the local Shona dialect. A related form—Zimbabwe—became the name of the country when it became free in 1980. Excavations at Great Zimbabwe have yielded many interesting artefacts, including a glazed Persian bowl, Chinese dishes and Arab coins minted in Kilwa, while recent genetic testing of a small local tribe has found DNA traces from Yemeni Jews. It seems quite clear that this kingdom probably had close trading relations with Indian Ocean ports like Kilwa.

The overwhelming evidence is that Great Zimbabwe was built and ruled by the local Shona people, even if ideas and influences were exchanged with the wider world of the Indian Ocean. However, colonial-era historians would insist that native Africans were simply not capable of building such elaborate stone structures and that this was the work of colonizers from the north. Under the racist government of Rhodesia (the British colony that became Zimbabwe), any research suggesting a native origin was deliberately suppressed. Colonial-era histories repeatedly stressed the idea that black Africans did not have a history till the Europeans arrived, as a means of serving their own ends. The truth, however, as we have seen, was quite different.

The Coming of the Central Asians

At the end of the twelfth century, the Indian Ocean rim could be divided into two zones of civilizational influence.

There was an Islamic zone that ran from Central Asia to the Swahili coast, and an Indic zone that ran from eastern Afghanistan to southern Vietnam. Further east, there was the Chinese civilizational zone that ran from the Gobi Desert to the Pacific Ocean, and included Japan, Korea and northern Vietnam. Although the exact borders of these zones shifted back and forth, it would have seemed to a casual observer of that time that a sort of equilibrium had been established. Unfortunately, this was about to unravel and all three civilizations would soon face a major shock. The source of their troubles was the same—the steppes of Central Asia.

India was the first to get a taste of what was to follow. Turkic invaders from Central Asia pushed out the Hindu Shahi rulers of Kabul and then began to make raids into India. Led by Mahmud of Ghazni, the Turks made as many as seventeen raids between AD 1000 and 1025 and destroyed and pillaged many of the prosperous cities and temple towns of north-western India. Perhaps the most infamous of these was an attack on the revered temple of Somnath in Gujarat. Fifty thousand of its defenders were put to the sword and some twenty million dirhams worth of gold, silver and gems were carried away. Somnath would be destroyed and rebuilt many times, but Mahmud's attack is still remembered most vividly. The temple that stands on the spot today was built in the 1950s. Its symbolic importance can be gauged from the fact that it was one of the first projects initiated by the Indian Republic. Despite the death and destruction caused by Mahmud, the Turks were unable to hold territory beyond some parts of western Punjab and Sindh. Indeed, an alliance led by Raja Suheldeo defeated a large Turkic army led by Mahmud's nephew at the Battle of Bahraich in 1033 (one version of oral history suggests Suheldeo was himself killed in battle). For a century and a half after this defeat, the Turks seem to have kept out of the heartlands.

To an Indian of those times, the Turkic raids would have seemed like yet another round of incursions like those of the Macedonians, Huns, Bactrians and Scythians of the past. The invaders had been either pushed out or absorbed, and had not posed a civilizational threat. If anything, there seems to have been a sense of complacency. So when Prithviraj Chauhan, ruler of Delhi, fended off a raid by Muhammad Ghori in 1191, he allowed the invader to return home to Afghanistan! Ghori returned the following year to defeat and kill Prithviraj. This led to the establishment of the Delhi Sultanate and opened up the rest of India to conquest. Over the next two centuries, the Turks would lay waste ancient cities, temples and universities in one of the most bloody episodes in human history. It is difficult to estimate exact numbers, but millions would have perished.

Bands of Turkic adventurers poured into India to seek their fortune. Bakhtiyar Khilji was one of these adventurers. He seems to have arrived in Ghazni from Central Asia around 1195 before moving to India as a soldier. He soon managed to get himself a small estate near Mirzapur (now in Uttar Pradesh) where he gathered a sizeable body of Central Asian soldiers of fortune like himself. Around 1200, Bakhtiyar attacked and destroyed the famous university of Nalanda. Most of the Brahmin scholars and Buddhist monks were put to death and its library was torched. Another famous university at Vikramshila was similarly destroyed soon thereafter. The common practice of Buddhism in India had been in steady decline, but it was still home to several institutions that attracted pilgrims and scholars from abroad. It now collapsed from the systematic destruction of these institutions. The Turks were unbelievably cruel towards Hindus and even fellow Muslims, but they seem to have reserved their worst for the Buddhists. One possible explanation for this is that they themselves had converted to Islam from Buddhism relatively recently and felt that they had to prove a point.

Encouraged by these successes, Bakhtiyar Khilji now decided to attempt the conquest of the wealthy kingdom of Bengal. Avoiding the usual routes, he led his army through the jungles of Jharkhand and made a surprise attack on Nabadwip, a pilgrimage town on the Ganga. It so happened that the ageing ruler of Bengal, Lakshman Sen, was visiting the town when a scouting party of eighteen Turkic horsemen was seen approaching the city. Taken totally by surprise, Lakshman Sen and his retinue escaped by boat. The popular version of this story is often told as if Bakhtiyar Khilji conquered Bengal with eighteen horsemen. In reality, the Sen dynasty would keep up an active resistance in East Bengal for another half a century by using the riverine terrain against Turkic cavalry.

After pillaging Bengal for two years, Bakhtiyar, it would seem, got bored. Ever the thrill seeker, he now decided to cross the Himalayas and conquer Tibet. He marched north and crossed the Teesta River by a stone bridge. He also asked the king of Kamrup (modern Assam) for troops and supplies. The Assamese king delayed, so an impatient Bakhtiyar decided to carry on by himself. The Turks raped and looted their way through the mountains of Darjeeling and Sikkim before entering Tibet. Here he faced stiffer resistance. With supply lines stretched, Bakhtiyar decided to retreat but his army was relentlessly harassed by guerrilla attacks as it made its way back through the mountain passes. Supplies were so short that the Turks were forced to eat some of their horses.

When the retreating army finally reached the Teesta, they found that the Assamese had destroyed the bridge and laid a trap. In the end, most of the Turks were killed by the Assamese or drowned in a desperate attempt to cross the fast-flowing river. Bakhtiyar escaped with only 100 of his men. Unfortunately for him, he had now lost his authority and was soon assassinated by one of his followers.

The death of Bakhtiyar Khilji, however, did not slow the Turks. In 1235, the great city of Ujjain, a major Hindu religious and cultural centre in Madhya Pradesh, was destroyed by the Delhi Sultanate. If the Turks were feeling smug about their successes in India, they were about to get a taste of their own medicine. The Mongols led by Chengiz Khan attacked and devastated the Turkic homelands in Central Asia in 1220–22. They soon conquered Iran and went on to sack Baghdad in 1258. The region would be ruled by Chengiz Khan's descendants for the next century and, despite the fact that Mongols were generally tolerant of different religions, for a while there was genuine concern that Islam would not recover from this shock. Interestingly, till they converted to Islam towards the end of their rule, the Mongol rulers of Iran were Buddhists or shamanists.

This Buddhist episode in Iranian history is now almost forgotten. Even as the Mongols were marching into the Middle East, they were simultaneously making inroads into China. Chengiz Khan captured the Yanjing (modern Beijing) capital of the northern Jin kingdom in 1215. However, the conquest of the southern Song Empire would be a long and bloody affair that would be completed by Chengiz's grandson, Kublai, in 1276. It is said that the last Song emperor, an eight-year-old boy, would die after jumping into the sea to avoid capture.

The rapid and simultaneous collapse of three established civilizations is difficult to explain merely on the basis of the tactical superiority of Turko-Mongol cavalry. All three civilizations had long experience of dealing with Central Asians. The popular perception in India is that the Hindus were unable to deal with a younger and more vigorous Islam. This too is inaccurate because Hindus had been dealing quite successfully with Islam for five centuries before Muhammad Ghori broke through. Moreover, the Turks did not conquer India during a period of glorious Muslim expansion but at a time when Islam itself was under severe stress in the Middle East and Central Asia. Were the established civilizations weakened by the equivalent of the Plague of Justinian in Asia? We know that the Black Death would devastate Europe and the Middle East in the following century, but did some such epidemic affect China and India in the thirteenth century? The available records are silent.

Whatever the reasons for the success of the Turks in India, the systematic destruction of temples did not just hurt intellectual and cultural life but also had a long-term paralysing impact on finance and risk-taking. As already discussed, temples acted as banks and their destruction meant that Indian merchant networks suddenly lost their financial muscle. Thus, we see a distinct decline in the importance of seafaring Indian merchants in the Indian Ocean rim from this point. The Indian merchant class became much more shore-based while the space they vacated was steadily taken over by Arabs and the Chinese. In other words, the Arabs and the Chinese recovered faster from the Turko-Mongol shock. In contrast, Indian Hindus imposed on themselves caste rules that discouraged the crossing of the seas. Why did a people with such a strong maritime tradition impose these restrictions on themselves? Was it a loss of civilizational self-confidence? I have long looked for a satisfactory answer but have not yet found one.

Nonetheless, I do not want to leave the reader with the impression that the Turks always had an easy time in India. Although they conquered the Gangetic plains with relative ease, they faced much stiffer resistance in other places. For instance, when they attempted to invade Odisha in 1247, the Turks were soundly defeated by Narasimha Deva I. It is said that the Odiya king pretended that he would embrace Islam and surrender the temple of Puri. However, while the Turks were celebrating their victory, the temple bells began to ring to signal a surprise attack by the Odiya army. The Odiya then chased the invaders back into Bengal. It is likely that the famous Sun Temple in Konark was built by Narasimha Deva I to celebrate this victory. At that time, Konark was a thriving port with links across the Indian Ocean. One of the temple's panels depicts the king, seated on an elephant, receiving the gift of a giraffe from a foreign ambassador!

Two Travellers' Tales

Perhaps the most vivid eyewitness accounts of these turbulent times have been left behind by two travellers— Marco Polo and Ibn Battuta. Marco Polo was born in 1254 to a Venetian merchant who made a journey to China around 1260. At the age of seventeen, Polo joined his father when he made his second journey in 1271. Over the next twenty years, the Polos would travel extensively in the Mongol Empire before returning to Venice. Several years after his return, Marco Polo would be captured in a war with Genoa and imprisoned. It was in prison that he dictated his book, *The Travels*, to a cellmate. The book is mostly remembered for its descriptions of the Silk Route through Central Asia and of Kublai Khan's empire in China, but it is often forgotten that Marco Polo returned home by the sea route and has left us many interesting observations about the Indian Ocean world.

He set sail in 1290 from the port Zaiton (Quanzhou) as part of a delegation accompanying a Mongol princess being sent to get married to the Mongol ruler of Persia. According to Marco Polo, the Chinese ships of the period were the largest in the world, with each containing 'at least sixty cabins' and with crews of up to 300 men. Polo tells us that as they sailed south, they stopped at the kingdom of Champa. A few years earlier, the Mongols had sent a large army to subdue the Chams who had stoutly defended their fortified cities. However, the devastation in the countryside had been so great that they had ultimately agreed to pay an annual tribute to Kublai Khan of aloe wood and twenty elephants. From Champa, they sailed in a south-westerly direction till they came to the island of Bintan (this is probably the Indonesian island of the same name, just south of Singapore). They then sailed up the Straits of Malacca along the eastern coast of Sumatra. It appears that Srivijaya had disintegrated by this time as Polo tells us that it was divided into eight independent kingdoms.

As they made their way into the Bay of Bengal, the ships stopped at the Nicobar Islands. Polo is quite disapproving of the fact that 'the people live like beasts. I assure you that they go stark naked, men and women alike, without any covering of any sort'. This is an obvious reference to the native population of the Andaman and

Nicobar Islands that, in some cases, have managed to maintain their hunter-gatherer lifestyles into modern times. However, note that this was a conscious preference rather than a lack of exposure to 'civilization'. Far from it, the heavy flow of mercantile trade past these islands meant that the Nicobarese were very familiar with things like cloth. Marco Polo tells us that the locals had acquired sashes of very high-quality silk that hung in their huts as a sign of wealth but steadfastly refused to wear them.

Marco Polo's ship now sailed across to Sri Lanka. Interestingly, he mentions that the island was once much larger and that part of it had been submerged in ancient times. Was this a medieval myth or a lingering memory of the Great Flood at the end of the last Ice Age? He next sailed north to India. Some of his accounts of the Indian coastline can be confusing at first glance as he mixes up the east and west coasts. Nevertheless, he relates some interesting anecdotes. For instance, he tells us that Indians were great believers in astrology and that business negotiations would often be suspended to avoid inauspicious times of the day. Polo also mentions that Indians had a peculiar way of drinking water—they poured the water into their mouths without the lips touching the cup. This way of drinking water still survives in parts of southern India!

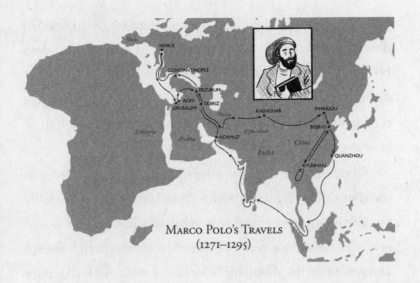

MARCO POLO'S TRAVELS
(1271–1295)

Till Marco Polo's time, India was almost the only source of diamonds. *The Travels* relates how the Indians acquired these gems. Evidently, the Indians claimed that there was a valley full of venomous snakes where the ground was covered in diamonds. The diamond merchants obtained the gems by—you guessed it—throwing large chunks of meat into the valley. The diamonds would stick to the meat that giant eagles picked up and carried to their nests. As one can see, the story mentioned by Herodotus and in *The Arabian Nights* was still circulating in the Indian Ocean! Marco Polo also mentions that the source of the diamonds was an inland kingdom ruled by a wise and popular queen. This is very likely a reference to Rudrama Devi, the queen of the

155

Kakatiya dynasty, who ruled over a kingdom that included the diamond mines of Golconda (just outside modern Hyderabad). She came to the throne in 1262 as her father did not have any sons. Although she married a Chalukya prince, she remained the ruler. Temple inscriptions tell us of how she personally led her armies to battle.

About half a century after Marco Polo, a Moroccan traveller called Ibn Battuta also visited India. He is arguably one of the greatest travel writers of all time, and he would eventually make his way to China before returning home to Tangier to write about his adventures. When Ibn Battuta visited India, the throne of Delhi was occupied by the somewhat erratic and intimidating sultan Muhammad bin Tughlaq. The Moroccan accepted a senior position in the sultan's government and spent about eight years in Delhi, before he was offered the opportunity to accompany a diplomatic mission to China, which he accepted.

Along with the rest of the embassy, Ibn Battuta made his way from Delhi to Gujarat and then to the port of Calicut. The old spice ports in Kerala were still thriving and crowded with foreign merchant ships. Ibn Battuta confirms Marco Polo's testimony about the enormous size of Chinese ships. He describes a large junk (a type of ship) that had a complement of 1000 men—600 soldiers and 400 sailors. When the sultan's embassy arrived in Calicut, most of the

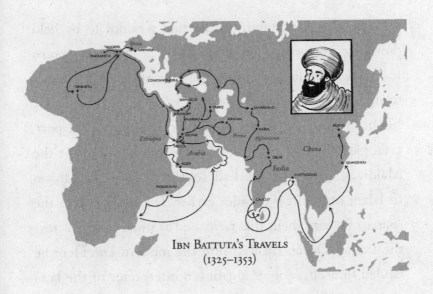

IBN BATTUTA'S TRAVELS
(1325–1353)

space on the ships had already been taken, owing to which Battuta hired a smaller vessel for himself. The evening before they were supposed to embark, a storm began to blow and the heavy surf meant that Ibn Battuta was unable to get on to the ship he had hired. The next morning, it was found that the large junk carrying the main embassy had been dashed on the shore and many had been killed. Meanwhile, the smaller ship containing the Moroccan's personal effects had decided to sail off without him! Thus, he suddenly found himself penniless and stranded in Calicut. He would try to desperately contact the surviving ship but later would find out that his personal goods and slaves had been seized by the authorities in Sumatra and sold off.

Ever the adventurer, Ibn Battuta was not to be held down by misfortune for long. He was afraid to return to Delhi as he did not know how the sultan would react to the news of the failed embassy. So, he joined the Turkic sultan of Honavar in his expedition against a rival port, even participating in the battle. He would later visit the Maldives, where people had converted from Buddhism to Islam only a few decades earlier. The islands were the source of cowry shells that were used as small change across the Indian Ocean till well into the modern era. Here he landed himself a job as a qadi (an interpreter of the law) and married a local woman but found that, despite the religious conversion, the natives did not follow the rules of Islam very closely, and writes that he tried to enforce these rules but without much success.

Ibn Battuta ultimately would give up on the Maldivians and make his way through Sri Lanka and South East Asia to China. It is a testimony to the active trade routes of the times that in China he would meet a fellow Moroccan whom he had previously met several years earlier in Delhi.

Marco Polo and Ibn Battuta may have been among the first to write down their experiences, but it is clear that they were using well-established networks used by many others.

CHAPTER 7

TREASURE ON THE OTHER SIDE OF THE WORLD

As the testimonies of Ibn Battuta and Marco Polo show, Indian Ocean trade networks survived the Turko-Mongol shock even if the relative importance of Indian merchants declined following this. The Mongols managed to extend their influence over Champa, but when they tried to extend it to Japan and Java, they were rebuffed. Meanwhile, the steady decline of Srivijaya in Sumatra meant that Java became the centre of political power in the region. Under the vigorous leadership of Kertanagara, the Javans extended their control over nearby islands like Bali and Madura. This expansion was briefly interrupted by a civil war when Kertanagara was assassinated by a usurper in 1292.

The murdered king's son-in-law, Kertarajasa, was organizing a revolt against the usurper when a Mongol fleet arrived from China with a large expeditionary force. Kertarajasa entered into an alliance with them and used them to recover the throne. If the Mongols were expecting the new king to become a grateful tributary, however, they were mistaken. Kertarajasa next turned on the foreigners and drove them away. He also established a new capital at Majapahit, the name by which his empire would be remembered. Kertarajasa was succeeded briefly by his son, who died without a son to follow him. The crown then passed to his eldest daughter and her line.

Around 1350, Kertarajasa's grandson Rajasanagara (also known as Hayam Wuruk) came to the throne. His long reign is remembered as the 'golden age' of the Majapahit Empire, but it was really his prime minister Gaja Mada who was the driving force. Under Gaja Mada's guidance, the Majapahit Empire established direct or indirect control over much of what is now the country of Indonesia. They grew so influential that they found themselves in conflict with the newly established Ming dynasty in China, whose rulers were now actively expanding their zone of influence.

The Chinese initially tried to establish independent relations with the smaller kingdoms of Sumatra, perhaps justifying this as a continuation of the old relationship between the Song and Srivijaya. The Majapahit, however, became alarmed when the Chinese sent an embassy to crown the ruler of Malayu in 1377. This was clear interference in the Majapahit sphere of influence. The Ming ambassadors were diverted to Java and killed. This resulted in a distinct cooling of diplomatic relations, and trade between China and South East Asia declined.

This is the background to the great voyages of Admiral Zheng He, which we will now look at.

The Treasure Fleet of the Dragon Throne

At the beginning of the fifteenth century, a new Ming emperor came to the throne and took the title of 'Yongle' (which means 'lasting joy'). At the very beginning of his rule, he decided to fund a series of grand voyages that would show South East Asia and the Indian Ocean rim just how powerful his empire was. These can't really be called voyages of exploration since Chinese ships had already been visiting these parts for centuries. Rather, they were an attempt to display geopolitical reach and to establish a system of tributes paid to the Ming Empire. Between 1405 and 1433, the Chinese fleet made seven voyages that included visits to Sumatra, India, Sri Lanka, Oman and the eastern coast of Africa.

No one who saw the fleet would have been left unimpressed. Leading the expedition were large junks called 'treasure ships' that had nine masts and were 400 feet long. To put this into context, Christopher Columbus's flagship, the *Santa Maria*, was only 85 feet long. The Chinese ships carried costly cargoes of porcelain, silk, lacquerware and other fine objects to be exchanged in trade or given as gifts to local rulers. Hundreds of smaller vessels accompanied the large treasure ships, including supply ships, water tankers, warships and so on. In total, as many as 27,000 sailors and soldiers were probably involved in each voyage.

ZHENG HE

The admiral who helmed these voyages was a Muslim eunuch of Mongol origin called Zheng He. He had been captured as a young boy when the Ming rulers evicted the Mongols from Yunnan province, and he was castrated before being presented as a servant to a prince. A bond of trust must have developed between the two boys because when that prince became Emperor Yongle, he put the young eunuch in charge of the Treasure Fleet.

The first fleet of 317 brightly painted ships set sail in the autumn of 1405 from Nanjing with a crew of 27,000 men. It made its way through South East Asia and stopped at Java, where Zheng He avoided a direct confrontation with the Majapahit Empire. This was his first voyage and he probably just wanted to gather information—and anyway, the sheer size of his fleet was enough to awe the locals. He also avoided Palembang, the old capital of Srivijaya, where a notorious Chinese pirate had established himself after evicting the Majapahit governor.

The Treasure Fleet next made its way to Sri Lanka. Zheng He noted the internal politics of the island but did not linger long before heading for the Indian port of Calicut. It had emerged as the largest port on India's west coast after Muzeris had been destroyed by a flood in 1341. The Chinese spent several months here trading their silks and porcelain for black pepper, pearls and other Indian goods. The fleet then headed back home. Off Sumatra, however, they engaged and destroyed the fleet of the Chinese pirate who had occupied Palembang. The survivors were taken back to China and executed.

Except for this skirmish, the first voyage was mainly one of information gathering. From now on, the Chinese would use the Treasure Fleet to move the chess pieces on the geopolitical board of the Indian Ocean. The second voyage set sail after only a few months. Its purpose was to return various ambassadors to their home countries but also to install a new ruler in Calicut. The ruler of Calicut, drawn from the matrilineal Nair warrior clan, was known as the 'Lord of the Seas' or Samudrin (also spelled Zamorin).

Chinese records suggest that they succeeded in installing their candidate. Although Indian sources are less clear about Chinese involvement, we know that during this decade, the Samudrins of Calicut expanded their power at the expense of rivals like Cochin (Kochi) and it is possible that Chinese support had something to do with it. It was also on the second voyage that the Treasure Fleet visited Thailand. In the early fifteenth century, the Chinese were looking to strengthen the Thai as a way to further weaken the declining empire of Angkor.

Over the next few voyages, Zheng He became increasingly confident as he gained experience. His fleet sailed widely from Bengal to the Swahili coast of Africa and then to the port of Hormuz at the mouth of the Persian Gulf. He also intervened systematically in local political rivalries where the opportunity presented itself in order to place compliant rulers on the throne. For instance, when the admiral visited Sri Lanka during the third voyage, he found that the island was in a state of civil war. The Chinese would capture at least one of the claimants to the throne and take him back to Nanjing to meet the Ming emperor. It appears that the Sacred Tooth Relic was also taken to China. Both would be sent back to Sri Lanka as part of a plan to ensure Chinese influence over the island. The Chinese would similarly intervene in a war of succession in the kingdom of Samudra in Sumatra.

However, the intervention with the most far-reaching historical implications was the support for the new kingdom of Melaka (also spelled Malacca) as a counterweight to the Majapahit Empire. The founder of Melaka was a prince called Parmeswara who claimed descent from the rulers of Srivijaya. He initially attempted to set up his base in Singapore but later decided to shift further north due to local rivalries and the continued fear of Javan attacks. The Chinese would provide him with systematic support from the very outset and we know that Parmeswara made at least one trip to China in order to personally pay obeisance to the Ming emperor. Interestingly,

Melaka was now encouraged to convert to Islam, possibly to create a source of opposition to the Hindu stronghold in Java. Melaka prospered under Chinese protection while the Majapahit Empire was steadily pushed back.

Meanwhile, back in China, the Treasure Fleets caused great excitement when they returned with ambassadors, goods and stories from faraway lands. The items that attracted the most curiosity, however, were giraffes that were seen as the 'qilin', mythical beasts that are considered sacred by the Chinese. The appearance of a qilin was seen to herald an age of prosperity and poems were written dedicated to the emperor and the giraffes. Problems were brewing, however, for Zheng He. The Confucian mandarins were increasingly suspicious of him and how powerful he was getting. So, after Yongle died in 1424, the mandarins steadily undermined the navy, which was under the control of Zheng He and his associates. After one last voyage in 1431–33, the treasure ships were allowed to rot and the records of the voyages were deliberately suppressed.

China then withdrew into isolation from which it eventually emerged only in the second half of the twentieth century. After this, it may have seemed that the Arabs would once more dominate Indian Ocean trade. But, as often happens in history, things took a rather different turn with the arrival of a completely new player—the Portuguese.

The Sun Sets on Angkor and Champa

The voyages of the Treasure Fleet may have stopped after 1433, but they had set in motion a chain of events that would fundamentally change the dynamics of South East Asia. After the Chinese had helped Melaka emerge as a rival to the Majapahit Empire, a Muslim alliance led by Melaka soon began to encroach into western Java. The empire steadily began to lose control over its spice ports. The Majapahit Empire would hold on to its heartland in eastern Java till the end of the century, but it was now clearly in decline. Many members of the Javan elite converted to Islam, while those who did not withdrew to the island of Bali in the early sixteenth century, where they have kept their culture alive to this day. Small Hindu communities such as the Tenggerese have also survived in Java, in the volcanic highlands around Mount Bromo.

The kingdom of Angkor, meanwhile, was under pressure from incursions by the Thai. The Thai were originally from southern China (Yunnan/Guangxi) but slowly encroached into the northern fringes of the Khmer Empire. By the middle of the fourteenth century, they had established a new capital at Ayutthaya (named after Ayodhya in India), not far from modern Bangkok. With the tacit support of the Ming Treasure Fleet, the Thai became increasingly aggressive and they sacked Angkor in 1431. The great city was eventually abandoned, although a much-reduced Khmer kingdom continued to survive. The Thai, however, would absorb many elements of the culture of Angkor—this is why much of what is now considered traditional Thai art and culture is of Khmer origin.

Even as the Khmers were being pushed aside by the Thai, their traditional Cham rivals were also facing a threat. For centuries, the kingdom of Champa had covered the southern half of Vietnam just as the kingdom of Dai Viet (literally Great Viet) had covered northern Vietnam. When Zheng He was embarking on his voyages, the Ming simultaneously invaded Dai Viet. Although initially defeated, the Vietnamese kept up a guerrilla war, which the Ming soon found too expensive to sustain. The Chinese were eventually squeezed out in 1428. The Viet spent the next couple of decades rebuilding their economy, but in 1446, they invaded Champa and briefly held its capital. In 1471, they returned in even greater force. Records suggest that 60,000 died in a last stand and that 30,000 captives were carried away (including the royal family).

Thus ended the kingdom of Champa that had lasted for one and a half millennia. It has left behind many enigmatic temples strewn across southern Vietnam. Sadly, the most important temple cluster in My Son was heavily damaged by American carpet bombing during the Vietnam War and, despite being designated as a UNESCO World Heritage Site, there is relatively little left to see. A small Cham community survives in Vietnam although many converted to Islam in the sixteenth century. Nonetheless, the tiny Balamon–Cham community (numbering around 30,000) still preserves a form of ancient Shaivite Hinduism in remote villages in southern Vietnam.

Why did these long-surviving Indianized kingdoms in South East Asia simultaneously collapse? Chinese intervention may have played a role, but it is arguably not the full story. By studying tree rings, researchers have found evidence that severe droughts and floods may have caused the complex hydraulic networks of Angkor to collapse in the fifteenth century. Java and Champa were also rice-based societies and it is likely that they too suffered from the same climatic fluctuations. Thus, it is possible that nature had a role to play in the collapse of these kingdoms.

The Amazing Exploits of Vasco da Gama

In the fifteenth century, some Europeans began to look for ways to trade with Asia directly. One option was to find a sea route to the Indies by sailing around Africa. The Portuguese took the lead and began to systematically sail down the west coast of Africa. In 1488, a captain called Bartholomew Diaz finally reached the southern tip of Africa. Most history books give the impression that the Portuguese then waited for a full decade before sending a fleet under Vasco da Gama to further explore the route. Given the importance of finding out more about this route, it seems unlikely that the voyage was casually postponed. There is evidence that suggests the Portuguese followed up Diaz's discovery with a number of secret voyages to properly document the winds and currents. After all, the Portuguese were quite suspicious of a certain Christopher Columbus who seemed to be sniffing around for information.

Tall tales

One of the intriguing aspects of the medieval world is the lack of accurate information the Europeans had about the Indian Ocean rim. Despite the accounts of occasional European travellers like Marco Polo, there was also a lot of misinformation, such as the fantastical tales of a character known as John Mandeville. Mandeville was an Englishman who left his country in 1322 and returned after thirty-four years, supposedly having travelled to China, India, Java and other places in the East. His account includes such creatures as one-eyed giants, women with dogs' heads and two-headed geese. He also embellished the widely held medieval European belief that there was a powerful Christian king called Prester John in India who would be a willing ally against the Muslims!

Around the same time as Diaz was making his way around Africa, King John II of Portugal had dispatched two spies disguised as Moroccan merchants to make their way to the Indian Ocean through the Red Sea in order to gather information on what the Portuguese fleet should expect after they rounded Africa. The two spies—Pero da Covilha and Afonso de Paiva—made their way to Aden where they split. The former would criss-cross the Indian Ocean for two years collecting information on various ports and kingdoms. Paiva, meanwhile, made his way inland to Ethiopia in the hope of finding the mythical Christian king Prester John. He would have been disappointed by what he saw. The Ethiopians had been surrounded by the Arabs for centuries and had somehow survived in isolation by retreating into the highlands.

After exploring the Indian Ocean, Covilha made it back to Aden and then to Cairo where he hoped to meet his companion. However, he soon realized that Paiva had died. He was preparing to return to Lisbon when he was contacted by two Jewish merchants carrying a secret message from King John II. The letter specifically asked for details on Prester John's kingdom. Covilha, therefore, sent back a report on the Indian Ocean ports with the merchants and decided to explore Ethiopia himself. He even made a risky detour to see Mecca for himself. When he finally reached

Ethiopia, however, the dowager Queen Helena refused to let him leave as he had learnt too much about the beleaguered kingdom's defences. Instead he was given a local wife and an estate (although he had a wife and estate back in Portugal) and asked to settle down. Thirty years later, a Portuguese emissary who came to visit found Covilha living the life of an Ethiopian nobleman!

After years of preparation, a Portuguese fleet under Vasco da Gama set sail in 1497 for India. Four years earlier, Columbus had returned from his voyage to the Americas but, thanks to all the intelligence gathering, the Portuguese seemed to have been quite confident that they were on the right track. Da Gama's fleet consisted of three ships—the *San Gabriel*, the *San Rafael* and the small caravel, *Berrio* (an additional store ship that accompanied them part of the way). They had a combined crew of 180 carefully selected men. The ships were also armed with cannons, which were not widely known in the Indian Ocean.

The fleet set sail on 8 July and arrived at the Cape of Good Hope by early November.

Although displaced from the rest of Africa by the Bantu, the Khoi-San were still the majority in the southern tip of the continent. They were not impressed by the newcomers and there was a skirmish in which da Gama was slightly wounded by a spear. After negotiating stormy waters off

Natal, the ships continued north, past the delta of the Zambezi. Here the fleet began to come across Arab dhows and settlements—Vasco da Gama now knew he was in the Indian Ocean!

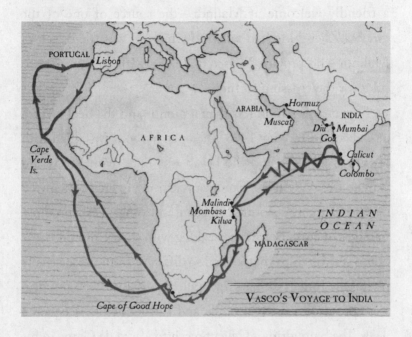

In order to keep their mission secret, the Europeans initially pretended that they were Turks and fellow Muslims. The Iberian peninsula had been recently freed from Arab rule and there were several Arabic speakers in da Gama's crew. However, the pretence soon broke down and the Portuguese narrowly escaped being ambushed by the sultan of Mombasa. The fleet now kept sailing up the Swahili coast, but news of their arrival seemed to have travelled ahead of them. Da Gama desperately needed a friendly harbour to replenish supplies and, most importantly, a pilot who could guide them across the ocean to India. At last, he received a friendly welcome at Malindi—the source of one of the giraffes Zheng He had taken to China. It was the sultan of Malindi who provided Vasco da Gama with an experienced pilot for the crossing to India.

The crossing took less than a month and the fleet arrived at Calicut on 14 May 1498. The open harbour was filled with vessels of all sizes and the beach was lined with shops and warehouses. When the Europeans arrived, many boats rowed up to sell them coconuts, chicken and other fresh produce. Families of curious sightseers, along with their children, came out to see the ships that looked so different from those usually plying the Indian Ocean. The opulent palace of the Samudrin was spread over a square mile and surrounded by lacquered walls. The Samudrin of Calicut received Vasco da Gama in his royal chamber, bare-bodied above the waist except for a string of pearls and a heart-shaped emerald surrounded by rubies, the insignia of royalty. Vasco da Gama knelt and presented a letter from King Manuel (John II's successor). He also laid out the gifts he had brought with him. The Samudrin was evidently not impressed with the gifts but agreed to trade in pepper and other spices in exchange for gold and silver.

The Arab merchants of Calicut were understandably unhappy to see their monopoly being broken. They even arranged to kidnap da Gama before he could return to his ship, but the Samudrin intervened and had him freed. The prosperity of Calicut depended on free trade and he had to ensure that the principle was upheld even if he felt uneasy about the newcomers. The Portuguese fleet, however, did not wait for long. After purchasing pepper, they lifted their anchors and headed home. Da Gama wanted to get home as soon as possible to tell his king about his discoveries. He received a rapturous welcome and was showered with honours and 20,000 gold cruzados. However, the human cost of the expedition had been great—two-thirds of the crew had perished during the voyage, including Vasco da Gama's brother.

Preparations now began for sending a much larger fleet to India. It would consist of thirteen ships armed with cannons and 1200 men under the overall command of Pedro Alvares Cabral. Despite the loss of some ships along the way, the fleet arrived in Calicut in September 1500 and demanded that the Samudrin expel all the Arabs and trade exclusively with Portugal. While prolonged negotiations were underway, a large Arab ship loaded with cargo and pilgrims decided to set sail for Aden. Cabral seized the ship and the Arabs retaliated by attacking a Portuguese contingent that was in the city. The Portuguese now seized ten more ships in the harbour and burnt their crew alive in full view of the people ashore. Next, they bombarded the city for two days and even forced the Samudrin to flee from his palace—a humiliation that the rulers of Calicut would never forget.

Thus began the European domination of the Indian Ocean. The fleet now headed south for Cochin (Kochi), a rival port that had lived in the shadow of Calicut since the time of Zheng He's visit. As had happened in the case of Malindi, the Portuguese would exploit a local rivalry in order to establish themselves. Cabral hurriedly loaded his ship with pepper and other spices, made payments in gold coins and headed home. Until then, pepper had usually made its way to Venice by the traditional Rea Sea route. This pepper cost 60–100 times its price on the Kerala coast. With the discovery of the new route, it was clear that Venice was ruined.

Using the profits from these successful voyages, the Portuguese now rapidly scaled up the number of fleets operating in the Indian Ocean. Within a couple of decades they had sacked or occupied many of the important ports in the western Indian Ocean region—Muscat, Mombasa, Socotra, Hormuz, Malacca and so on. Even by the standards of that time, they established a reputation for ruthlessness. For example, when Vasco da Gama returned on a second voyage to Calicut, he refused to negotiate and simply bombarded the city for three days. He also seized all the ships he found in the harbour and their crews—800 men in all. They were paraded on ships' decks and then killed by having their arms, noses and ears amputated. When the Samudrin sent a Brahmin to negotiate for peace, he was gruesomely mutilated and sent back. His two sons and a nephew, who had accompanied him, were hanged from the mast.

In other words, the maritime world of the Indian Ocean rim now experienced a shock similar to what had been experienced by the inland cities of Asia during the Turko-Mongol invasions. The Islamic world clearly needed to respond and it fell to the Turks to provide a comeback. The Ottoman Turks were the most powerful Muslim empire of that time and had taken Constantinople (i.e., Istanbul) in 1453, thereby ending the last vestige of the Byzantines (the Eastern Roman Empire). They had recently developed naval capability in the Mediterranean. However, they were aware that their galleys were not capable of dealing with the much more demanding conditions in the Indian Ocean. The traditional vessels of the Arabs were also deemed unsuitable as the stitched ships could not take the shock wave from firing cannons. Thus, twelve large warships were custom-built on the Red Sea and fitted out with cannons.

Interestingly, Venice provided the Turks with inputs from their spies in Portugal and even put a team of gunners at the sultan's disposal. The Turkish fleet sailed down the Red Sea in early 1507 under the command of Amir Husayn and headed for the Indian coast. Together with reinforcements sent by Calicut, the Turks won a battle against a small and unprepared Portuguese fleet anchored at Chaul (near modern Mumbai). The Portuguese were enraged and a large fleet was assembled. The two sides met near the island of Diu, just off the coast of Gujarat in February 1509. In the battle that followed, the superiority of European ship and cannon designs was fully displayed. Within hours, Husayn's defensive line had been shattered and the Turks were forced to flee. An additional factor that helped the Portuguese was the fact that the forces sent by the sultan of Gujarat remained neutral, rather than helping the Turks.

Despite these victories, the Portuguese still operated like nomadic pirates and did not have a permanent establishment in the Indian Ocean yet. After another unsuccessful raid on Calicut, it was decided that Goa would be a good place to build a base. Under the command of Afonso de Albuquerque, the Portuguese attacked and took Goa from the sultan of Bijapur in 1510. Soon, the Portuguese built a network of fortifications around the Indian Ocean rim from where they controlled their maritime empire. Perhaps the best preserved of these forts can be seen today on the island of Diu. The fort would fend off a second Turkish attempt against the Europeans in 1538.

A Story of Friendship and Swashbuckling Adventure

Better technology may partly explain Portugal's success, but it was also driven by the fact that its expeditions attracted extraordinary adventurers, who were ruthless and willing to take enormous personal risks. Two such characters were Ferdinand Magellan and Francisco Serrao, close friends who would participate in the first Portuguese attempt to capture Malacca in 1509. Magellan would later become famous for having led the first successful circumnavigation of the globe (although he would be killed in the Philippines and would not complete the voyage himself). Serrao is now almost forgotten, but his story is just as fascinating as Magellan's.

The first Portuguese attack on Malacca ended in defeat and Serrao narrowly escaped with his life thanks to a last-minute rescue by Magellan. Two years later, he returned as part of a large fleet under the personal command of Afonso de Albuquerque. The Malaccans put up a spirited defence but were eventually overcome. Albuquerque then ordered the construction of a new fort on a natural hill overlooking the town. Meanwhile, Serrao was made captain of one of three ships sent out to scout the Spice Islands further east.

Although his ship was leaking badly, Serrao somehow made it to the Banda Islands, the world's only source of nutmeg. While the other ships loaded nutmeg, Serrao purchased a Chinese junk as a replacement for his ruined ship. It tells us something about the man's self-confidence that it was manned with a crew of just nine Portuguese and a dozen Malays. On the return journey, however, a storm separated the three ships. Serrao's junk was blown into a reef and he lost several of his men. The survivors were now marooned on a small uninhabited island with no water. Nonetheless, Serrao kept his cool and took care to retrieve his guns before hiding his men in the undergrowth in anticipation of local pirates who might come to investigate the wreck.

MAGELLAN'S
SHIP

Francisco
Serrao

Ferdinand
Magellan

Sure enough, a boatload of pirates arrived and, at a pre-decided signal, the Portuguese party rushed to the beach and captured the pirates and their boat. The survivors now headed for the nearest inhabited island of Hitu. The chiefs of this island were at this time at war with a nearby island and Serrao decided to impress them by joining in a surprise attack. There were only a handful of Portuguese guns, but the defenders were totally unused to them and were routed. Serrao and his band of merry men returned as heroes to Hitu and their fame spread to nearby islands. While they were celebrating their victory, a flotilla of war canoes arrived with an invitation from the sultan of Ternate.

The twin volcanic islands of Tidore and Ternate were the world's only source of cloves, but their rulers were bitter rivals. Serrao must have already heard of them and he accepted the invitation. News of Portuguese victories in the Indian Ocean had clearly reached these parts, for Serrao was received like royalty when he reached Ternate. He soon established himself as the sultan's right-hand man. When a Portuguese fleet finally reached the island a couple of years later, the captain was amazed at Serrao's influence and lavish lifestyle. They seethed in envy at a colleague who they saw as a renegade and deserter who had gone native. For the moment, however, they recognized that Serrao's unique position was an advantage and he was allowed to continue.

Serrao sent back letters to his superiors as well as to his friend Magellan, whom he urged to join him in the Spice Islands. These letters were what inspired Magellan with the idea that Ternate and Tidore were so far east that they could be accessed easily by sailing west from the Americas. The problem was that the Portuguese authorities were not keen on exploring an idea that could provide the Spanish with easy access to the Spice Islands. So, Magellan took his plans to the Spanish who agreed to fund his expedition.

In March 1521, after sailing around South America and enduring many hardships, Magellan's fleet managed to reach the Philippines. When the Spanish landed on the island of Cebu, the area was ruled by a Hindu dynasty of possibly Tamil origin. Magellan signed a treaty with Raja Humabon and converted him to Catholicism. This is the basis on which the Spanish would later claim the islands. One of Humabon's vassal chiefs Lapulapu, however, refused and the Spanish were obliged to demonstrate their military superiority. It is not known why Magellan decided to storm Lapulapu's island personally, but it is possible that he was trying to live up to Serrao's exploits. In any event, he was surrounded and killed on the beach.

Magellan's remaining fleet, however, continued on its voyage and a few weeks later anchored at Tidore. Here they heard that Serrao had died a few weeks earlier, possibly poisoned by local rivals. It is amazing how close Serrao and Magellan had come to achieving their rendezvous on the other side of the world. Only one ship from Magellan's fleet with twenty-one survivors would make it back to Spain. Its cargo of cloves was valued at 10,000 times what it had cost in Tidore.

Thus ended a story of friendship and swashbuckling adventure.

The Inquisition Comes to India

One of the enclaves acquired by the Portuguese during the sixteenth century was Bombay, then a collection of marshy islands. The sculpted caves of Elephanta Island suggest that the area had been an important commercial hub in the seventh and eighth centuries, but had since declined. The first Portuguese landing on the islands was in 1509; over the next few decades, the Portuguese managed to establish a small enclave here. One of its earliest European residents was Garcia da Orta, a physician and naturalist, who would spend decades quietly studying the medicinal properties of local herbs and their use by Indian and Arab doctors. His best-known work is *Colloquies on the Simples and Drugs of India*, first published in Goa in 1561. The treatise would turn him into a national hero in Portugal. This is ironic, as Garcia was living quietly in this remote outpost because he wanted to stay away from the authorities in Lisbon!

In order to understand why, we need to go back to 1492 when the Spanish ended Moorish (North African) rule in the Iberian peninsula and ordered all Jews and Muslims to leave. Those who remained behind were forced to become Christians, and were known as New Christians. However, the authorities suspected that these New Christians were continuing to practise their old religions in secret. It was to hunt them out that the dreadful Spanish Inquisition originally began. Garcia da Orta's parents were Spanish Jews who had fled to Portugal to escape being imprisoned and killed. Unfortunately, a few years afterwards, the Portuguese too ordered all Jews to leave. In fact, Vasco da Gama's voyage had been partly funded by the wealth taken away from the Jews before they had been told to leave. The Orta family remained in Portugal by ostensibly converting to Catholicism, but they were always afraid of being investigated by the Inquisition.

There is evidence that the Ortas continued to practise Judaism in secret and this is the real reason that Garcia da Orta was living quietly in Bombay. Over time, he used his contacts in the colonial headquarters in Goa to bring over family members and other New Christians from Portugal. In this way, Goa and other Portuguese enclaves ended up with a sizeable New Christian population. Although there was always an air of uncertainty, things were tolerable till the arrival of Francis Xavier, a Jesuit missionary, in 1542.

Xavier, later to be canonized as a saint, is known today in India for the numerous Jesuit schools and colleges named after him. However, it was he who invited the Inquisition to come to Goa before leaving for Malacca. When the Inquisition arrived in Goa, the vast majority of the local population practised Hinduism. Egged on by the Jesuits, the Portuguese destroyed temples, and killed or forcibly converted local Hindus to Christianity. The remains of destroyed temples can still be seen in Goa, and, in recent years, a handful of these have been rebuilt by local Hindus. The Inquisition soon turned on the communities of Syrian Christians who had lived peacefully on India's west coast for over a thousand years before the arrival of the Portuguese. Their ancient rituals were condemned as heretical and they were forced to accept Latin rites; many of their books and records composed in Syriac were burnt. Not surprisingly, the Inquisition also began to scrutinize the New Christians. Many would be tortured and killed including Garcia da Orta's sister Catrina who was burnt at the stake as 'as an impertinent Jewess' in 1569, a year after Garcia's death. Her husband confessed under torture that the famous physician had kept 'the Sabbath on Saturday'. It is a reflection of the vindictiveness of the Inquisition that Orta's remains were dug out of his grave and burnt, and the ashes thrown into the Mandovi River.

The City of Victory

When the Portuguese first arrived in India, most of the northern and central parts of the subcontinent were ruled by rulers of Turkic, Afghan and Persian origin (although there remained several others, such as the rulers of the kingdom of Mewar). The southern half of the Indian peninsula, however, was home to a remarkable Indian empire remembered today by the name of its capital—Vijayanagar. Built on the banks of the Tungabhadra River, it was then the largest city in the world. The city is said to have been established in 1336 by two brothers Hukka (also called Harihara) and Bukka in the aftermath of Turkic raids that destroyed the old kingdoms of southern India. It is said that Hukka and Bukka began to gather together and organize the shattered remains of the defeated armies. Very soon they were able to establish control over a sizeable kingdom.

As anyone who has visited Hampi will know, it is a strange landscape of rocky outcrops and low hills. Hukka and Bukka probably realized that this terrain would offer them good defences against invaders. Many foreign visitors have left us eyewitness accounts of how the city looked in the fifteenth and sixteenth centuries. Abdul Razzaq, an envoy from the Timurid ruler of Persia, wrote that the city had seven concentric walls that enclosed a vast area that included cultivated fields and gardens, homes, grand temples, workshops and bustling bazaars. At the centre was the royal citadel that contained the palace and the grand assembly hall. Razzaq tells us that rock-cut aqueducts and canals brought water from the river to the palace complex. The remains of the city at Hampi are truly spectacular and are comparable to those at Angkor, except that the dense Cambodian jungle is replaced here by gigantic rock outcrops littered across the landscape. A fair amount of agriculture continues to be practised within the UNESCO World Heritage Site, in many cases using the medieval canal system.

HAMPI

Once the Portuguese established themselves on the Indian coast, a number of Europeans also visited Vijayanagar and have left us detailed accounts. These include horse-traders Domingo Paes and Fernao Nuniz who wrote about Vijayanagar under Krishnadeva Raya, arguably the greatest of its rulers. They describe the grand feasts, dancing and ceremonies that accompanied the Mahanavami festival. They also describe life in the court. Interestingly, Nuniz tells us that women dominated the palace complex, including 'women who wrestle, and others who are astrologers and soothsayers; and women who write all the accounts of expenses that occurred inside the gates, and others whose duty is to write all the affairs of the kingdom and compare their books with the writers outside; women also for music who play instruments and sing'.

Krishnadeva Raya was a vigorous military leader and he personally led several campaigns against the Deccan Sultans. The Portuguese horse-traders were awed by the sheer size of the Vijayanagar army. Interestingly, we are told that the armies, both of Vijayanagar and of the Deccan Sultans, included significant numbers of European mercenaries who were valued as gunners and musketeers. Although not explicitly mentioned, we know that these armies would also have included units of African slave-soldiers. Muslim rulers had long used slave-soldiers, but it appears that Vijayanagar and the Portuguese also adopted the practice. A few of them, like the Ethiopian-born general Malik Ambar, would rise to hold high office.

The African diaspora in India

The descendants of these Africans survive today as the tiny Siddi community in Karnataka, Hyderabad and also in Gujarat. They usually adopted the culture of the rulers they served—so in the former territories of the Vijayanagar empire, they are now mostly Hindus while further north, they are mostly Muslims or Christians. Recent genetic tests have confirmed that Siddis are mostly derived from the Bantu-speaking people of East Africa.

The great city was eventually sacked and abandoned just a few decades after Krishnadeva Raya's death. In 1565, a grand alliance of all the Deccan Sultans marched against Vijayanagar. After a closely fought battle at Talikota, 100 kilometres north of the city, the Vijayanagar army was forced to retreat. The generals decided to withdraw south rather than protect the capital and its formidable defences were not put to the test. The largest city in the world was pillaged for six months and never recovered. A much diminished kingdom survived for several decades more, but the authority of the king steadily faded away.

The Warrior Queens of Ullal

The Portuguese had been hot and cold with Vijayanagar, but the empire's decline opened up large sections of the Indian coast for exploitation without restraint. Even before the battle of Talikota, the Portuguese had been sniffing around for a base on the Kanara coast (this is the stretch between Goa and Kerala). Their efforts were thwarted, however, by the remarkable warrior queen of the tiny kingdom of Ullal near Mangalore. She belonged to the Chowtha dynasty that were of Gujarati Jain origin but had adopted the matrilineal customs of the region. Tradition decreed that a king's successor was his sister's son, but Thirumala Raya did not have a nephew. So, he decided instead to train his niece Abbakka to succeed him. Although she married the ruler of nearby Mangalore, she remained in Ullal as its ruler.

In 1555, the Portuguese sent a fleet under Don Alvaro da Silveira to subdue Mangalore and Ullal. While Rani Abbakka and her husband may not have gotten along, they seem to have joined forces and fended off the attack. Both kingdoms were nominally ruled by Vijayanagar and the Portuguese decided not to press the issue and agreed to a truce—for a while. For they decided to try their luck once again, after Vijayanagar was defeated at Talikota. A large fleet was dispatched from Goa in 1567 under the command of General Joao Peixoto. The city of Ullal and the palace were captured, but the queen managed to stay hidden in a mosque. She then gathered 200 of her men and organized a counter-attack in which scores of Portuguese, including Peixoto, were killed. Abbakka now chased the survivors back to their ships where Admiral Mascarenhas was also killed.

Over the next fifteen years, Abbakka seems to have held the Kanara coast with the help of an alliance with the Samudrin of Calicut to the south and the sultans of Bijapur to the north. But the Portuguese waited for their chance and returned in 1581 with the help of Abbakka's husband's nephew, who had become the ruler of Mangalore. This time Ullal was sacked and Abbakka was sadly killed in battle. However, Abbakka's daughter and then her granddaughter would keep up the resistance for the next four decades using light coastal vessels to strike at the larger European ships. They were the last known users of fire arrows in naval warfare.

There is surprisingly little written by scholars about the three queens, although their exploits are well remembered in the oral histories of the Kanara coast and are recounted in numerous folk songs and in dance theatre. The problem is that the folk tales often combine the three queens into one character, which makes it difficult to work out exactly who did what. The warrior queens are also mentioned in a few

European accounts such as those of Pietro della Valle, but we still only have scraps of information that have not quite been pieced together. So, a full history of the remarkable queens of Ullal is yet to be written.

CHAPTER 8

IN SEARCH OF SPICES

Although the sixteenth century was dominated by Spain and Portugal, their supremacy would be challenged before the century was over by two newcomers—the Dutch and the English. In 1580, the English sea captain Francis Drake returned to England after circumnavigating (travelling all the way around) the world. He brought back two things: one, a ship filled with Spanish booty and spices from the Indies, and two, information that the Portuguese hold on trade in the Indian Ocean region was not as secure as widely believed.

The English now decided that it was time to stake a claim on the spice trade. A fleet of three ships was sent out under the command of James Lancaster in 1591. The ships bypassed India and made directly for the Straits of Malacca. The English did not even pretend to trade but simply plundered Portuguese and local ships before heading back. On the way home, however, two of the three ships were wrecked in a storm and all the ill-gotten cargo was lost. The smallest of the three ships somehow limped back with just twenty-five survivors, including Lancaster himself.

In the meantime, the Dutch also sent out a number of fleets, which brought home much valuable cargo. Spurred on by this, English merchants decided to take another shot at sailing eastwards. Queen Elizabeth I was petitioned for a royal charter, a document that granted a right or power to a person or a group. On New Year's Eve in 1600, the merchants set up as 'The Company of Merchants of London trading into the East Indies'; we know this now as the East India Company (EIC). Dutch merchants similarly banded together to form the United East India Company (also known by its Dutch initials, VOC).

Both of these entities would grow to become among the largest and most powerful multinational companies the world has ever seen.

The Extraordinary Life and Death of Nathaniel Courthope

In February 1601, the English East India Company (EIC) sent out its first fleet of four ships, once again under the command of James Lancaster. Again, the fleet bypassed India and headed directly for South East Asia, this time landing in Aceh, on the northern tip of Sumatra. The English were received with great warmth by the sultan, who hoped that they would provide a counterbalance to Portuguese naval power in the region. The English fleet then made its way down the Straits of Malacca, pillaging Portuguese ships on the way to Java. The Dutch already had a settlement in Java, at Bantam, from which they could control the alternative route through the Sunda Strait. Much to their annoyance, the local ruler allowed the English to also set up a base in the same area. Soon, the English were using Bantam to send ships out to the spice-growing islands further east. In 1610, an English ship made its way to the nutmeg-growing Banda Islands. When the ship arrived at the main island of Neira, it found that the VOC had already arrived and imposed a monopoly on the locals.

Faced with Dutch hostility, the English decided instead to trade with two tiny outlying islands—Pulau Ai and Pulau Run—where the locals had thus far resisted Dutch pressure. Pulau Run consisted of a mere 700 acres of nutmeg plantations and did not even have enough water or rice to sustain its small population. The local chiefs were so afraid of the VOC that they threw themselves under

English protection. Thus, Ai and Run became the first colonies of the English East India Company. However, the English soon discovered that their claim on the islands had to be actively defended against the VOC and the young governor general of the Dutch East Indies, Jan Pieterszoon Coen. In 1616, the English sent out two ships under the command of Captain Nathaniel Courthope, to the Bandas in order to establish a permanent presence. Young Captain Courthope and his men landed a battery of brass cannons on Pulau Run and proceeded to build a small fort using exposed coral rock. The Cross of St George was proudly flown from it, a move that would have surely annoyed the Dutch.

Despite this act of defiance by the English, it soon became clear that the Dutch had the muscle to impose a blockade on Pulau Run. As the months rolled by, supplies began to run low for not just the English garrison but also for the locals. Using local traders, Courthope sent back increasingly desperate appeals for help to his superiors in Bantam, but the attention of East India Company's commanders was unfortunately taken up with internal bickering and by a siege of the new VOC headquarters at Batavia (Jakarta). When the siege failed, most of the English fleet sailed home—without sending relief to Pulau

Run. Thus, the blockade on Nathaniel Courthope and his men tightened. When a feeble attempt was eventually made to resupply them, the Dutch were easily able to block it. Matters became worse when the rains failed in 1618. The island's water reserves were precariously low and the water teemed with so many tropical parasites and worms that it had to be drunk through clenched teeth. Three and a half years passed this way, during which disease and poor nutrition slowly depleted the English garrison. It is a testimony to the young captain's leadership that the dwindling English troops and their Bandanese allies were able to fend off repeated Dutch attempts to land troops on the island.

Eventually, things became so desperate that Courthope decided to risk making a trip to a nearby Dutch-held island in order to secure food supplies from sympathetic islanders. Unfortunately, his small boat was discovered and he was killed. However, his men and local allies continued to hold out till Coen arrived with a huge fleet in April 1621. His first targets were the Bandanese on Dutch-held islands, whom he accused of violating the VOC monopoly. Of the 15,000 islanders, barely a thousand survived death or deportation. Many of those deported to Batavia would be tortured and killed. Coen now turned his attention to Pulau Run where a dozen English soldiers were still holing up. When 500 VOC soldiers landed on the island, these Englishmen finally surrendered. This was the end of the EIC's first colony.

PULAU RUN, 17TH CENTURY

Coen continued to systematically tighten his control over the East Indies by using brutal tactics to terrorize both European rivals and the native population. In 1624, fifteen Englishmen based in Ambon, in the Maluku Islands, were tortured and decapitated on trumped-up charges. Known as the Ambon Massacre, it caused a furore in England. In 1641, the Dutch evicted the Portuguese from Malacca and thereby secured control over both the routes to the Spice Islands. The heroic resistance of Nathaniel Courthope, nevertheless, had established a territorial claim that would have a curious unintended consequence. When England and Holland signed the Treaty of Breda in 1667, they agreed to swap two islands—the Dutch got Pulau Run in the East Indies in exchange for the somewhat larger island of Manhattan in North America!

The Rise of Madras, Bombay and Calcutta

Besides their rivalry with the Dutch, the East India Company's other major problem in South East Asia was that there were few takers for English goods. As a result, the English constantly coughed up bullion (gold) in exchange for spices. This was the same problem that the Romans had faced 1500 years earlier. However, the EIC soon discovered that South East Asia had an insatiable demand for Indian cotton textiles and that they could make a profit by participating in intra-Asian trade. Soon, they also found a market for Indian textiles back in Europe. Thus, more than black pepper, textiles were the reason that the EIC decided to build permanent establishments in India.

The English soon set up modest warehouses in Machilipatnam on the Andhra coast, Hugli in Bengal and Surat in Gujarat. As business grew, the EIC decided that it was necessary to build fortified settlements that could be defended against both Indian rulers as well as European rivals. The first of these was Madras (now Chennai). A small strip of coastline was acquired from the local ruler in 1639 by the EIC agent Francis Day. It was an odd choice as it was neither easily defensible nor did it have a sheltered harbour. Ships had to be anchored far from the shore and boats had to ferry people and goods through heavy surf. It was not uncommon for boats to overturn and cause the loss of life and property. Nonetheless, the English built a fortified warehouse here and christened it Fort St George.

The next major settlement was Bombay, which was acquired from the Portuguese as part of the dowry when King Charles II married Catherine of Braganza. The group of small islands was leased to the EIC in 1668 for ten pounds per annum. Unlike Madras, it already had a small but functioning settlement and also a good harbour. As a naval power, the English would have found its island geography easier to defend and a more substantial fort was built on the main island, in the area still known as 'Fort'. A series of smaller fortifications were also maintained at various strategic points.

The third major EIC settlement was built in Bengal. Yet again, the decision was taken because the English found their position in the old river port of Hugli untenable due to conflicts with the Mughal governor. When peace was finally declared after an abject apology from the English, they were allowed to return and set up a new establishment. In 1690, the EIC's agent Job Charnock bought the rights to three villages from the local landlords for 1300 rupees. This is how Calcutta (now Kolkata) was founded. The English soon built Fort William—this is not the star-shaped eighteenth-century fort that is used today as the Indian Army's eastern headquarters but its predecessor, which was built on the site now occupied by the General Post Office. Nonetheless, the proximity of the Mughals and later the Marathas made the EIC directors in London nervous. The humid, swampy terrain, moreover, took a heavy toll on the Europeans and even Job Charnock died within three years of founding the outpost. It is worth mentioning that each of the above EIC settlements soon attracted a sizeable population of Indian merchants, clerks, labourers, sailors, artisans, mercenaries and other service providers. Thus, Madras, Bombay and Calcutta each developed a thriving 'black town' where the Indians lived.

The English were not the only Europeans building trading posts during this period. The French East India Company, a relative latecomer, would build a number of outposts including a major settlement in Pondicherry (now Puducherry). This was established right next to the Roman-era port of Arikamedu. Pondicherry would remain a French possession till the 1950s and still retains a strong French flavour. My own favourite example of a European settlement from this era is the Danish fort in Tranquebar (Yes, even the Danes were in the game!). Tranquebar (or Tharangambadi) is south of Pondicherry and very close to the old Chola port of Nagapattinam. It was here that Danish admiral Ove Gjedde built Fort Dansborg in 1620, well before the English and French forts. Despite this early start, the Danish East India Company was never able to make a success of its operations in the Indian Ocean and Tranquebar sank into obscurity.

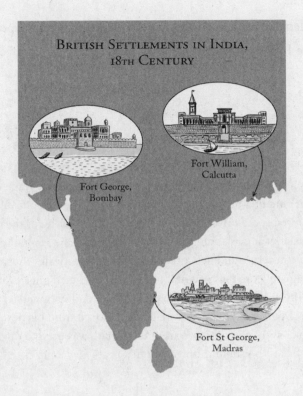

BRITISH SETTLEMENTS IN INDIA, 18TH CENTURY

Fort George, Bombay

Fort William, Calcutta

Fort St George, Madras

The Pirate Avery and Aurangzeb's 'Granddaughter'

The building of these settlements may give the impression that the various East India Companies were thriving and wealthy, but the reality was that they made big profits in some years but large losses in others. Wars, shipwrecks and fluctuations in commodity prices affected trade significantly. And then, towards the end of the seventeenth century, a new problem arrived in the form of European pirates operating in the Indian Ocean.

Private trade

One of the perennial problems the EIC faced was that its employees were often more interested in their private trade than in pursuing the company's larger interest. The EIC officially allowed some private trade in order to compensate for the low salaries it paid, but its agents often misused the company's infrastructure and networks to further private deals. Thus, the company bore the costs and individuals pocketed huge profits. This is how Elihu Yale, the governor of Madras, amassed a large personal fortune before being removed from his post on suspicions of corruption. Part of this wealth was used to fund the prestigious university that bears his name.

The origins of these pirates lay in what was called privateering, a culture that thrived in the Atlantic. Different European monarchs granted commissions to private parties to carry out acts of piracy against rival states. The English, for instance, used privateers to great effect against the Spanish in the Caribbean. However, once this culture of piracy had been established, it was not long before well-armed European pirates began to expand their operations into the Indian Ocean, with many using Madagascar as a base. One of the most successful of these pirates was a man named Captain Henry Avery, also known as Henry Every or John Avery.

Born in Plymouth, England, Avery had served as a junior officer in the Royal Navy. In 1693, he signed up for a privateering expedition aimed at French shipping in the Caribbean and was assigned to the forty-six-gun flagship. The owners of the ship, however, did not pay the crew on time and Avery led a mutiny that took over the ship and renamed it the *Fancy*. Using the ship's firepower, Avery and his men looted and pillaged their way across the Atlantic before heading for the secluded harbours

HENRY AVERY
1659–1699

of Madagascar. The original mutineers had been British, but Danish and French sailors, who had volunteered to join the pirates, had been added to the crew along the way. They now set their sights on the shipping that passed between India and the Yemeni port of Mocha (it was famous for its coffee exports).

The *Fancy* headed for Bab-el-Mandeb but when it arrived there, it found small sloops, also flying English colours, waiting for the Mocha fleet. These were privateers from Rhode Island and Delaware with licences to raid enemy shipping in the Atlantic, but who had also decided to try piracy in the Indian Ocean. Seeing the *Fancy's* firepower, they agreed to work for Avery and the group hunted like a pack of wolves over the next few months. One of the ships they captured was the *Fath Mahmamadi*, which belonged to the wealthy Surat merchant Abdul Gafoor and yielded 50–60,000 pounds worth in gold and silver!

Just two days later, the pirates came across the enormous *Ganj-i-Sawai*, owned by Mughal emperor Aurangzeb himself. The ship was heavily armed and confidently prepared to put up a fight. However, as the battle began, one of the Mughal cannons exploded and killed several of the ship's gunners. Just then, the *Fancy* fired a full broadside that knocked over the main mast of the *Ganj-i-Sawai* and turned the main deck into a disarray of rigging and sail. Amidst the confusion, the pirates boarded the crippled ship and took it over.

The story goes that the ship was carrying the stunningly beautiful granddaughter of the Mughal emperor. Avery, it is said, immediately asked for her hand and, on receiving her consent, married her on board the captured ship. Her beautiful handmaidens were similarly married off to various members of the pirate crew. In reality, the pirates subjected the passengers and crew to a great deal of violence, which induced several women on board to kill themselves by jumping into the sea. The treasure the pirates found on the *Ganj-i-Sawai* is said to have been worth 1,50,000 pounds in gold, silver, ivory and jewels. Avery and his crew took their share of the booty and headed to Nassau in the Bahamas, where they too split up. Some of the pirates were later caught, but the captain himself simply vanished, thus becoming a legend. For the next couple of decades, rumours would circulate among the world's sailors that Avery had made his way back to Madagascar, where he lived with his Mughal princess. This legend inspired a whole new generation of pirates.

Perhaps no one suffered more from all this piracy than Abdul Gafoor, the wealthiest merchant of Surat and owner of the largest trading fleet in the Indian Ocean. He repeatedly complained to the Mughal authorities who, in turn, accused the European companies of aiding the pirates. After the *Ganj-i-Sawai* incident, the Mughal governor of Surat demanded that the Dutch and English East India Companies provide ships to patrol the Mocha–Surat passage. The Europeans were also forced to pay compensation to Indian merchants who lost their ships to European pirates. Sustained pressure did eventually have some impact on piracy and several pirates, including Captain Kidd, were executed in the early eighteenth century.

The Portuguese and the Merchant's Daughter

The seventeenth century brought with it one of the most important powershifts of the era: the decline of Portuguese power. This was partly due to the entry of other Europeans in the Indian Ocean and partly due to the fact that local rulers adopted cannons and learnt to deal with European military tactics. In 1622, the Portuguese lost Hormuz to the Persians and shifted their base to Muscat in Oman. This was defended by two mud forts—Mirani and Jalali—both built on craggy rock outcrops overlooking the harbour. Despite the shift to Muscat, the Portuguese found that their position was not secure. Led by Imam Nasir ibn Murshid, the Omanis had regrouped in the interiors and were steadily reclaiming the coastline. By the time Murshid died in 1649, the Portuguese had lost all their other possessions and were left holding on to only Muscat. Murshid was succeeded by his cousin, the equally aggressive Sultan ibn Saif, who wanted to capture even this last outpost. Unfortunately, this proved difficult because as long as the Portuguese controlled the harbour, they could resupply themselves from Goa.

Legend has it that the Portuguese depended on an Indian merchant called Naruttam to supply their provisions. He had a beautiful daughter whom the Portuguese commander Pereira coveted. Naruttam and his daughter were not keen on the match, but Pereira kept up the pressure. At last, under threat, the merchant agreed and requested some time to prepare for a grand wedding. Meanwhile, he convinced the authorities that Mirani Fort needed to be cleared out so that he could do some repairs. Using this as the pretext, Naruttam removed all the provisions from the fort and then informed Sultan ibn Saif that the garrison was unprepared for a siege. The Omanis attacked immediately and took the fort and the town in 1650. Thus, an Indian father's determination to protect his beloved daughter may have led to the demise of the Portuguese in Oman.

Meanwhile, in India, the Portuguese were squeezed out by the Mughals and later by the Marathas. Pushed out of their base in Hugli, they were reduced to piracy in Bengal and withdrew to Chittagong where they formed an alliance with the Arakanese king Thiri, with whom they carried out raids into the riverine delta of Bengal. The Portuguese had also established themselves in Sri Lanka and had built a strong base in Colombo. They even managed to baptize Dharmapala, the ruler of the nearby kingdom of Kotte (effectively a suburb of Colombo and now the official capital of the country). This success, however, led to growing resentment when Dharmapala confiscated all the lands owned by Buddhist and Hindu institutions and gifted them to the Franciscans.

When Dharmapala bequeathed his kingdom to the Portuguese crown, the simmering anger rose and a Sinhalese resistance was led by Rajasimha, the ruler of a rival kingdom, who united a sizeable part of the island under his rule before turning on the foreigners. Although he repeatedly pushed the Portuguese back to Colombo, he was unable to take the fort because it could be continuously resupplied by ship from Goa. After Rajasimha, however, the Sri Lankan resistance collapsed and the Portuguese were able to expand control over much of the coastline. The Sinhalese now withdrew to mountain strongholds around Kandy. They became even more isolated when the Portuguese took over the Tamil kingdom in Jaffna, thereby cutting off communications with traditional allies in southern India.

Given its difficult situation, it is not surprising that the Kingdom of Kandy entered into an alliance with the Dutch in 1638. Together they evicted the Portuguese from Sri Lanka. However, as the Sinhalese may have feared from the beginning, they had only exchanged one foreign colonizer with another. Over the next century, the Dutch would use their base in Sri Lanka to slowly expand control over the Indian coast, especially the pepper ports of Kerala. Perhaps the VOC dreamt that in the long run it could extend control over large parts of India as it had done in Indonesia. However, the world's most powerful multinational company was thwarted by the remarkable Marthanda Varma, ruler of the small kingdom of Travancore in the southern tip of India.

The Battle of Colachel

Marthanda Varma was born into the royal family of Travancore and, as per the matrilineal custom of the Nair clan, he inherited the crown from his maternal uncle in 1729 at the age of twenty-three. His problem was that the Dutch tightly controlled the pepper trade on which the prosperity of Kerala depended. The locals were unable to put up any resistance because the region was divided into very small kingdoms. Even within the kingdoms, the king had limited say as power was dispersed among the Nair nobility. Rather than rely on the old feudal levies, Marthanda Varma began by building a standing army drilled in modern warfare. He also began to take over neighbouring kingdoms one by one.

Not surprisingly, the rulers of these kingdoms appealed to the Dutch who repeatedly warned Travancore. Eventually, the VOC governor of Ceylon dispatched a sizeable force of Dutch marines that landed at the small port of Colachel and marched on the royal palace in Padmanabhapuram in 1741. Marthanda Varma was away but returned in time to defend his capital. The Dutch were now chased back to Colachel where they suffered a humiliating defeat. The Battle of Colachel was a turning point and Dutch power in the Indian Ocean would go into steady decline. Not till the Japanese navy defeated the Russians in 1905 would another Asian state decisively defeat a European power.

Marthanda Varma's palace at Padmanabhapuram still survives and is an excellent example of Travancore's traditional wooden architecture. It also contains a painting showing Marthanda Varma accepting the surrender of the Dutch commander Eustachius de Lannoy.

PADMANABHAPURAM PALACE

Interestingly, the king offered to hire Lannoy as a general provided he trained his army on European lines. The Dutch captain accepted the offer and would loyally serve Travancore for over three decades. He would not just modernize the army but also build a network of forts using the most advanced European designs of that time. The army trained by Lannoy would help Travancore further expand the kingdom to as far north as Cochin (Kochi) and would help break the Dutch monopoly. Half a century later, it would help Travancore defend itself against Tipu Sultan of Mysore. For his energetic leadership, Lannoy would earn the title of 'Valiya Kapithaan' or Great Captain from his men. One can visit his grave at Udayagiri Fort that he built not far from the royal palace. The inscription is both in Latin and Tamil, a fitting reflection of his dual identities.

Britain vs France

While the Dutch were being squeezed by Travancore, the English and the Portuguese were up against another source of indigenous resistance. After the death of Mughal emperor Aurangzeb in 1707, the empire had quickly unravelled and a large part of it was taken over by the Marathas. In 1712, Kanhoji Angre was appointed the Surkhail or Grand Admiral of the Maratha navy. Often dismissed as a pirate in European writings, he was a legitimate official of the Maratha Empire. When the English resisted, he detained a number of EIC ships and forced them to pay a fine. He did the same to the Portuguese. The reason Angre was able to impose his will on the Europeans was that the Marathas had learnt to challenge them at sea. A favourite tactic was to use smaller but fast and manoeuvrable vessels to approach a European ship from astern in order to avoid the cannon broadside. Sometimes, they would also tow a larger cannon-laden vessel that would direct its fire at the sails and rigging in order to disable the ship. While the European gunners were trying to extricate themselves from the tangle of rope and canvas, the faster Maratha boats would close in and board the ship.

The EIC initially agreed to Angre's demands but were soon found to be violating various conditions. Accusations and counter-accusations flew thick and fast, and Bombay began to prepare for war. A large fleet was assembled in 1718 and sailed down to Angre's main base at the fortress of Vijaydurg. The attack was a total failure and the siege was lifted after just four days. The English and the Portuguese would try repeatedly to capture Vijaydurg over the next few years without any success. Eventually, the EIC called for help from the Royal Navy and in 1722, Vijaydurg was attacked by the large combined fleet of the EIC, the Royal Navy and the Portuguese. Yet again, the attackers failed to make a dent and were forced to withdraw. Except for the English, the Europeans would make their peace with Angre one at a time.

Kanhoji Angre died in 1729, but his descendants would harass the EIC for the next two decades. The internal politics of the Marathas, however, came to the EIC's rescue. In 1756, Vijaydurg found itself under siege with the EIC fleet blockading it from the sea and the Marathas from land. The fort and its harbour fell after heavy bombardment from land and sea, effectively ending Maratha naval power.

By the middle of the eighteenth century, with the Portuguese and Dutch in decline, the British had emerged as the strongest naval power in the Indian Ocean. However, the directors of the EIC still baulked at the idea of a land empire, and it was the French, their main rivals, who first attempted to control inland territory. The key person behind this was Joseph Francois Dupleix, the governor of Pondicherry. At this time, the British and the French were at war in Europe, but their companies in India had initially refrained from attacking each other. This changed when a British fleet plundered French ships in the Straits of Malacca in 1745. Dupleix immediately requested support from the French naval base in Mauritius. When reinforcements arrived the following year, the French marched on Madras and captured it without much difficulty. The EIC now complained to the Nawab of Arcot, the Mughal governor of the area (although by this time the Mughal Empire was rapidly dissolving). The Nawab arrived in Madras with a large force but was decimated by French cannon.

With the largest British settlement under his control and the Indians in awe of his firepower, it would have seemed that Dupleix was in a position to dramatically expand the French territory. However, he was repeatedly undermined by his colleagues and superiors. In 1749, he was forced to hand back Madras to the British as part of a peace deal in Europe. Dupleix was not yet done; within a year, he had managed to place his own candidates as rulers of Hyderabad and the Carnatic coast. As the Maratha navy was being tamed on the west coast, the French seemed to have taken control of the east coast.

The two European companies now began to prepare for war and both recruited a large number of Indian soldiers and drilled them in modern warfare. What followed was a series of engagements known as the Carnatic Wars. The mounting cost of these wars would eventually force the French to recall Dupleix. Meanwhile, the British hand would be strengthened by a decisive victory over the ruler of Bengal. Anyone with even a passing interest in Indian history would have heard of the Battle of Plassey in 1757 where British troops led by Robert Clive defeated Siraj-ud-Daulah, the Nawab of Bengal. Clive had 800 European soldiers, 2200 Indian sepoys and a contingent of artillerymen. The Nawab's army had 35,000 infantrymen, 15,000 cavalry, 53 cannons and also a small French contingent. This would appear like a big numerical advantage except that a large segment of the Nawab's army, led by Mir Jafar, did not take part in the battle. The French contingent put up some resistance, as did the men led by two loyalists Mir Madan and Mohanlal. However, unsure of how many troops he still controlled, Siraj-ud-Daulah fled the battlefield (later he would be captured and killed). Mir Jafar became the new Nawab of Bengal, but it was Robert Clive who was truly in charge. This is how the East India Company came to control a major chunk of Indian territory.

The Many Faces of Tipu Sultan

Despite their success in Bengal and control over the sea, the British were far from being the masters of India. The Marathas remained the biggest threat to their hegemony for another half a century till they were finally defeated in the Third Anglo-Maratha War of 1817–18. The East India Company also had to contend with the hostility of a number of other rulers such as Tipu Sultan, the ruler of Mysore.

Tipu Sultan came to the throne in 1782 after the death of his father Hyder Ali. Hyder Ali had taken over the throne of Mysore from the Wodeyar dynasty that he had served as a military commander. Over the next few years, Tipu crushed all dissent within his kingdom as well as took over the smaller kingdoms adjoining Mysore. The Karnataka coast and the

Kodavas of Coorg (now Kodagu in Karnataka) soon found themselves under savage assault. Around 1788, Tipu Sultan turned his attention on the Kerala coast and marched in with a very large army. The old port city of Calicut was razed to the ground. Hundreds of temples and churches were systematically destroyed and tens of thousands of Hindus and Christians were either killed or forcibly converted to Islam. This is not just testified by Tipu Sultan's enemies but in his own writings and those of his court historian Mir Hussein Kirmani.

Following this, hundreds of thousands of refugees began to stream south into Travancore. Tipu now used a flimsy excuse to invade the kingdom founded half a century earlier by Marthanda Varma. Travancore's forces were much smaller than those of Mysore, but Lannoy had left behind a well-drilled army and a network of fortifications. Tipu's army was repeatedly repulsed by the Nair troops, but Travancore knew that it was up against a much larger military machine and was forced to ask the EIC for help. The British responded by putting together a grand alliance of Tipu's enemies that included the Marathas and the Nizam of Hyderabad and, in 1791, they marched on Mysore. Within a few months, the allies had taken over most of Tipu's kingdom and were bearing down on his capital Srirangapatna. Eventually, he was forced to accept humiliating terms—half his kingdom was taken away and he was made to pay a big war indemnity.

Friendless in India, Tipu now began to look for allies abroad. It is known that he exchanged letters with Napoleon and had great hopes of receiving support from the French. He also wrote to the Ottoman sultan in Istanbul and urged a joint jihad against the infidel British. The problem was that Napoleon had occupied Egypt and the Ottomans considered the French the real infidel enemies and the British as allies! British intelligence was fully aware of what Tipu was doing and decided to finish him once and for all. The allies again marched on Srirangapatna in 1799. The Mysore army was a shadow of its former self and the allies had little difficulty in reaching the capital. After three weeks of bombardment, the walls were breached. Tipu Sultan died fighting, sword in hand. And the allies would restore Mysore to the old Wodeyar dynasty. Tipu's personal effects were taken by the victors and most of them were shipped to England where they can be seen in various museums.

Napoleon's nemesis

Napoleon may have done little to rescue his ally, but the siege of Srirangapatna would bolster the reputation of a thirty-year-old British colonel named Arthur Wellesley. Now remembered as the Duke of Wellington, he would defeat Napoleon sixteen years later at Waterloo.

Since his death, Tipu Sultan has been painted both as a heroic figure and as a cruel villain. It is true that, despite the intolerance he displayed towards Hindus and Christians in Kerala and Coorg, there are also several instances of his making generous grants to temples. While he cannot be called a freedom fighter, it is important to remember that, as with most historical figures, he was at best some shade of grey.

CHAPTER 9

THIS LAND IS OUR LAND

Despite not being able to expand into India, the VOC retained control over Sri Lanka and much of South East Asia till the end of the eighteenth century—until something happened to destroy the Dutch monopoly.

Over the years, attempts had been made to grow Asian spices outside their places of origin. Pepper, originally from south India, had spread to Sumatra and elsewhere, but cloves and nutmeg had proved impossible to grow outside their original habitats. Moreover, the Dutch jealously guarded against any attempt to smuggle out seedlings so as to retain their monopoly. The first attempt at transplanting these spices was made by Pierre Poivre, a French adventurer and later administrator of Mauritius. Poivre personally captained a ship to the Spice Islands and procured a small number of seedlings. Unfortunately, the plants did not survive for long in Mauritius.

A few years later, Poivre sent out a man called Provost to attempt to procure seedlings. Sailing through VOC-controlled waters, the French managed to find a small island where the locals, unknown to the Dutch, had succeeded in transplanting clove and nutmeg. Provost procured seedlings from them before heading for Mauritius, but was caught by Dutch customs officials. However, the French managed to convince the officers that they had been blown off course and escaped a full inspection. Provost returned to Mauritius with 400 rooted nutmeg trees and seventy rooted clove trees. Within a couple of decades, there were spice plantations in Zanzibar, Madagascar and the Caribbean. With its spice monopoly shattered, the VOC's fortunes went into rapid decline. The company was dissolved in 1799.

The Free Port of Singapore

Meanwhile, the English East India Company was facing a problem. It had succeeded on the battlefield and acquired control over territory, but its operations in India were not very profitable. Even as its agents became rich through unscrupulous dealings, the company suffered. By the late eighteenth century, trade with China was the only profitable part of the EIC's operations. However, the Chinese insisted on being paid in silver coins in exchange for tea, porcelain and other products coveted in Europe. Soon, the British faced the same precious metals shortage the ancient Romans had faced when trading with India.

The EIC's directors found their solution in opium. Opium had been imported in small quantities into China from ancient times and used in traditional medicine. From the late eighteenth century, however, it became very fashionable to smoke it, and it began to be consumed at all levels of society. As demand for opium boomed, the British found that they could use their control over India to grow poppies. Indian farmers in EIC-controlled areas were forced to grow opium (along with indigo that was used as a dye) and sell it to company agents at artificially low prices. And so, a system of triangular trade was born. The British sold cheap mill-made textiles to the Indians and bought opium from them for very cheap prices. The opium was then sold to the Chinese in exchange for goods that were sold in Europe. Cheap textiles made on an industrial scale by British mills devastated India's artisan-based textile industry, and the poor returns from opium cultivation impoverished farmers, but what made it worse was that they were often not free to grow food crops; even small fluctuations in weather conditions therefore resulted in devastating famines.

Although this system solved the precious metals issue, the British were still exposed to other kinds of risks. The sea route from India to China had to pass through the Malacca Straits and there was always the risk that the Dutch would use their control over the region to cut off access. So, when Napoleon took control of Holland, the British moved systematically to take over Dutch territories in the Indian Ocean. Since their home country was under occupation, the Dutch put up little resistance. By 1799, the VOC itself ceased to exist; by 1811, the British (whose troops included many Indian soldiers) took over the Dutch headquarters at Batavia (Jakarta) and occupied Java. It was also a column of Indian troops led by a young officer called Thomas Stamford Raffles that marched into central Java and stormed the palace of the sultan of Yogyakarta. Raffles returned to England briefly before coming back as the governor of the tiny British colony of Bencoolen in Sumatra. When Napoleon was defeated in Europe, he realized that the Dutch would ask the British to return their territories in the Indian Ocean, putting the sailing route to China through the Malacca Straits at risk. Raffles thus identified Singapore as a good place to set up a new outpost that would ensure permanent British control over the passage.

Raffles managed to gain control over the island in 1819 and declared that Singapore would be a free port. The idea of a free port under British protection was immediately attractive and, within a few weeks, thousands of Malays and

Chinese had shifted from Malacca to Singapore; the city was a bubbling mix of cultures right from the beginning. The Dutch were furious and lodged a protest with London claiming that the free port was within their traditional zone of influence. However, the new settlement became so successful in such a short time that it could not be ignored. The authorities in London and Calcutta grasped its strategic importance at the tip of the Malay Peninsula and eventually backed Raffles. The Dutch, in any case, were too weak to push their case too far. The Anglo-Dutch Treaty of 1824 gave the British control over Singapore and the Malay Peninsula, including Malacca. The Dutch regained the territories that we now know as Indonesia. As compensation for Singapore, the Dutch also got Bencoolen.

Dutch Sri Lanka Turns British

The Dutch territory of Sri Lanka was also occupied by the British during the Napoleonic wars. While the Europeans had taken control of the coast, the mountainous interior was still under the kingdom of Kandy. The kingdom was then ruled by the Nayak dynasty, who were not Sinhalese but were of south Indian origin. The Nayaks were aware of their foreign status and they strongly encouraged a Buddhist revival in order to cement their position. By the eighteenth century, the institutions of Buddhism had long been in decline due to constant wars and the pressure from Christian missionaries. The Nayak kings, therefore, brought over monks from Thailand to re-establish various institutions.

Meanwhile, having secured the coast, the British decided to attempt what both the Portuguese and the Dutch had failed to do—subjugate Kandy. In May 1803, an expeditionary force was sent into the mountains but on arrival found that the town had been evacuated. While the commanders were debating what to do next, the monsoons arrived and the British found themselves caught without supplies in a muddy and wet terrain. Eventually, they decided to retreat to Colombo but were harassed constantly by Sinhalese guerrilla attacks as they made their way back through the slushy mountain passes. Almost all the British officers and men were killed. The British returned to Kandy in 1815 and, taking advantage of frictions between the king and the nobility, took over the kingdom with little resistance. Thus, the whole of Sri Lanka became part of the British Empire.

The Haze of Opium

Chinese authorities strictly restricted the flourishing trade with the Europeans to a single port—Canton (i.e.,

Guangdong). Business was controlled by a cartel of wealthy Chinese merchants known as the Hongs. During the trading season (September to January), Europeans were allowed to stay in the port in lodgings leased out by their Hong counterparts. Situated deliberately outside Canton's city walls, these 'factories' included warehouses and living quarters. Outside of the trading season, the foreigners were expected to either go home or withdraw to the Portuguese enclave of Macau. Despite these restrictions, the East India Company and its agents benefited from cosy long-term relationships with the Hongs. But after the EIC's business rivals in Britain lobbied hard, the company's monopoly over trade with the East ended, and many new merchants arrived to try and sell opium in China. Even the Americans entered the business. Many of the new entrants began to bypass the old arrangements and smuggle the drug into the mainland. As a result, the price of opium fell and its usage rose sharply in China. The flow of silver coins reversed and opium addiction became widespread.

The Chinese imperial government was eventually forced to take action and, in May 1839, the authorities confiscated and destroyed 20,000 chests of opium in Humen, triggering a chain of events that resulted in the First Opium War. The British sent out fifteen barrack ships backed by the *Nemesis*, a steam-powered warship.

The scattered and outdated Chinese army was completely outmatched as the British fleet pounded its way up the coast. Ultimately, the Manchu emperor was forced to accept the humiliating conditions of the Treaty of Nanjing by which several ports were forced open for foreign trade and the British gained control of Hong Kong. War reparations, including compensation for the confiscated opium, were also paid.

The peace between the Chinese and the British soon broke a few years later. Tensions began to simmer in 1856 but the British could not respond for the next couple of years because a large section of the British-Indian army was in revolt across northern India during 1857–58. Given the importance of Indian soldiers in policing the growing empire, the British were able to pay attention to China only after the revolt had been brutally suppressed. The Second Opium War started as a series of skirmishes, and a large expeditionary force was finally dispatched in 1860. With the active support of the French and the Americans, the British repeatedly defeated the Chinese imperial army and marched into Beijing. The Qing emperor fled his capital and the Summer Palace was deliberately destroyed. Yet again, Indian troops formed the bulk of British forces. It seems clear that the British Empire was heavily dependent on Indian soldiers to enforce its authority.

The Tycoons of Bombay

Despite its successes, the East India Company was in trouble by the middle of the nineteenth century. Incessant wars, rampant corruption and, ultimately, the loss of its monopoly had steadily eroded the company's profits. The Revolt of 1857–58 in India exposed its inability to govern the empire it had created. After the revolt, the EIC's colonies were taken over by the British Crown. Even as the EIC's fortunes declined, it was replaced by new merchants and agency houses, one of the largest of which was Jardine, Matheson & Company (which survives today as the conglomerate Jardine Matheson Holdings). It was set up by Charles Magniac, James Matheson and William Jardine who initially used technical loopholes to circumvent the EIC's monopoly in order to trade Indian cotton and opium in exchange for tea out of Canton. Business boomed after the EIC lost its monopoly in 1834 and they relocated their operations to Hong Kong after the First Opium War.

While most Indian farmers and weavers were hurt by the triangular trade system, some Indians also benefited from it, including many from the Parsi community. The Parsis were descendants of Zoroastrian refugees who had come to India centuries earlier from Iran. From the late eighteenth century, many Parsis had migrated to Bombay where they prospered as suppliers, victuallers (sellers of alcohol) and shipbuilders. Opium exports were initially monopolized by Calcutta, but Bombay gradually emerged as an alternative hub as cotton farmers in Malwa switched to growing opium. Soon, Parsi agents became an important part of the supply chain all the way to Hong Kong.

Arguably the most successful of the Parsi merchants of Bombay was Jamsetjee Jeejeebhoy, born in 1783. Bombay was a much smaller settlement than Calcutta but, with the Maratha threat receding, it now witnessed rapid growth. In 1780, the population of Bombay was estimated at 47,170, but by 1814 it had risen to 1,62,570 and had further jumped to 5,66,119 by 1849. Armed with a smattering of English and some knowledge of bookkeeping, the enterprising Jeejeebhoy soon inserted himself into the city's trading community, steadily earning himself both a large business and a good reputation as a reliable partner.

In 1805, a few months before the British decisively beat the French navy at Trafalgar, Jamsetjee and William Jardine met when they were both taken captive by the French. The captors later agreed to release the prisoners at a neutral Dutch outpost near the Cape of Good Hope at the tip of Africa. While this transfer was taking place, a sudden gale wrecked their ship near the Cape. Both Jamsetjee and Jardine survived, but the shared experience created a bond that became the basis of a long-term business partnership. Jamsetjee soon became the main Indian partner of Jardine, Matheson & Company and acquired a large fleet of ships. He also became a highly respected citizen of Bombay and was included by the EIC's Court of Directors in the Queen's Honours List, and was knighted in May 1842.

The incredible luxury of ice cream

One of Jamsetjee's lesser-known contributions to Mumbai is the introduction of ice cream. This was made possible by the regular supply of ice from Boston from the 1830s. An icehouse was built to store the ice, but the stock often ran out due to melting or delays in the supply chain. Not surprisingly, the rich saw ice as a way to display their wealth and Jamsetjee began to serve ice cream at his dinner parties. The very first time he served it, it was alleged that everyone caught a cold!

Another of Bombay's merchant princes was David Sassoon, a Baghdadi Jew who had fled the despotic rule of Daud Pasha. When Sassoon arrived in Bombay in 1833, the city already had a significant Jewish population. He soon built a business empire trading in cotton and opium, but the Sassoon family fortunes skyrocketed when the American Civil War cut off supplies of raw cotton between 1861 and 1865. The mills of Lancashire turned to India for raw material and Bombay witnessed a boom. David Sassoon died in 1864 but he is remembered through several institutions built by him and his sons in Mumbai and Pune. Sassoon's palatial house survives as Masina Hospital in the neighbourhood of Byculla. The David Sassoon Library, built in Mumbai's Kala Ghoda area, is another elegant example of the period's architecture. The Sassoon Docks in Colaba were built by David's son Albert Abdullah. It is now used to land Mumbai's daily supply of fish.

Not all of Bombay's tycoons made their money from opium. Premchand Roychand would make, lose and regain his fortune in real estate and financial markets. His father had brought his family from Gujarat and had settled in a tenement in the densely packed Kalbadevi area. By the 1850s, Roychand had amassed a sizeable capital base as a cotton broker. Around the same time, a small group of Indian brokers began to trade financial securities and bullion under a banyan tree in front of Town Hall (this later evolved into the Bombay Stock Exchange). It was in this milieu of speculation and risk-taking that Premchand Roychand began to promote land reclamation projects.

By this time, the original seven islands of Bombay had already been connected through land reclamation into a single land mass, but growing population and commercial activity argued for further reclamation. What added fuel to the fire was the cotton boom caused by the American Civil War. Investment in reclamation shot up. Soon, the city saw many new banks, companies and construction projects being launched and Premchand was involved in several of them. It was mania like never before and, inevitably, it all came crashing down when North American cotton supplies resumed in 1865. Many investors were ruined in the aftermath and the economic collapse was so large that the city's population dropped from 8,16,000 in 1864 to 6,44,000 in 1872!

Premchand Roychand not only lost everything but was also blamed for the wider financial mess. Nonetheless, he seems to have been stoic about the whole affair and, over the following decades, would repay those he owed money to and gradually build back his fortune. When he died in 1906, he would be remembered for his extraordinary resilience and the large sums he gave away to charity and public works. For instance, the Rajabai Clock Tower, one of Mumbai's most iconic buildings, was built with funding from Premchand Roychand and is named after his mother.

RAJABAI CLOCK TOWER

The stories of these three tycoons give a good sense of how Bombay evolved and expanded over the nineteenth century. These were larger-than-life figures who took big, even reckless risks but were also prepared to share their good fortune. Sassoon, Jamsetjee and Premchand were all migrants who had made it big in the city. Mumbai's slums are still full of migrants who think they too can do it.

This is why Mumbai slums are not places of hopelessness as one may expect but full of industry and enterprise.

A Ceremonial Banquet Goes Horribly Wrong

Even as the Europeans were tightening their stranglehold on the Indian subcontinent and South East Asia, the Persian Gulf was witnessing big changes too. As we saw in the previous chapter, the Omanis had managed to evict the Portuguese in the mid-seventeenth century but a few decades later, they found themselves under occupation by the Persians led by Nadir Shah (the same Nadir Shah who raided Delhi in 1739 and captured the famous Peacock Throne).

In 1747, Ahmad ibn Said united the various feuding Omani factions and then invited the Persian officers for a ceremonial banquet. At a signal given midway through the meal, the hosts suddenly attacked and massacred the guests. The occupying Persian forces were left leaderless and were pushed out with ease. Nonetheless, the Omanis knew that they remained under threat and therefore opted for a long-term strategic alliance with the British. The British, in turn, were keen on building up a local alliance as a bulwark against the Wahhabis of the Arabian Peninsula. In 1804, Sultan Said came to the throne. His fifty-two-year rule is often seen as a 'golden age' by the Omanis. His success was based on the gradual building up of naval power. Using his growing fleet, and with implicit British support, the Omanis steadily expanded control over a maritime empire that extended from Gwadar on the Makran coast (now in Pakistan) to Zanzibar off the East African coast (now in Tanzania).

The economic engine of the empire was powered by cloves grown in Zanzibar and African slaves procured from the interiors. This meant that Sultan Said needed to maintain control over the Swahili coast. Much of this coastline had been explored and settled by the Omanis in medieval times and some links had been intermittently maintained. In the 1830s, the Omani court moved to Zanzibar and tightened its grip. The trade in slaves, however, was eventually abandoned under pressure from the British. The Omani nobility would continue to rule over Zanzibar till as late as 1964 when a revolution would overthrow them. Many would be killed in riots and most of the remaining Arabs would leave. Zanzibar would then merge with Tanganyika on the mainland to form Tanzania. The island's once thriving Indian community was also hurt by the revolution and most left for other shores.

Steamships and Fishing Fleets

From the middle of the nineteenth century, coal-powered railways and steamships dramatically reduced the time taken to move goods and people over land and sea. These also changed the dynamics of naval war with the construction of steam-powered, armour-plated, iron-hulled warships. The other major factor that changed the dynamics of the Indian Ocean was the Suez Canal. As we have seen, the idea of a canal was not new and various versions had been built since ancient times. However, all the earlier versions had focused on connecting the Red Sea to the Nile and, in each case, were choked by sand and silt after a few years. In contrast, the nineteenth-century canal built jointly by the French and the Egyptians and opened in 1869 connected the Red Sea directly with the Mediterranean. The Egyptian partners eventually sold their stake to the British. Combined with steam power, the Suez Canal soon changed the logistics of Atlantic–Indian Ocean trade as ships no longer had to make the long and arduous journey around Africa.

One of the less anticipated effects of the Suez Canal was the flood of young, unmarried European women who headed for India and other colonies in search of husbands. Known as the 'fishing fleet', these women were drawn from all segments of society. Depending on their social background, they would marry British civilian and military officers, merchants, clerks and so on. Some even found their way into the harems of native princes. The arrival of so many women transformed the Europeans in Asia into a ruling caste that lived in enclaves with conventions and etiquette completely separate from those of the indigenous people.

Meanwhile, ships also carried increasing numbers of Indians across the Indian Ocean and beyond, but their experience was very different. A key factor driving this churn of people was the shortage of labour in sugar-growing colonies after the British abolished slavery in 1833. Within a year, there were fourteen ships engaged in transporting Indian indentured workers from Calcutta to Mauritius. An indentured worker is a worker who signs a contract that binds him or her to a particular employer for a fixed period of time. The original contracts were for five years at ten rupees per month plus some food and clothing. An option of a free return passage was provided at the end of the contract.

SUEZ CANAL

Soon, Indian indentured workers were being transported to faraway places like Mauritius, the Caribbean and Fiji. Other European countries, such as France, also began to recruit workers. By the 1840s, the authorities began to encourage women to sign up so that self-perpetuating Indian communities could be created, which in turn would reduce the need for constant replenishment from the mother country. The recruitment of indentured workers was done by a network of Indian subagents who further contracted out their work. The whole supply chain was riddled with false promises and rampant abuse, but repeated famines in India pushed increasing numbers to risk the journey. In 1870–79 alone, Calcutta shipped out 1,42,793 workers, Madras 19,104 and Pondicherry 20,269.

Indentured workers and soldiers were not the only Indians on the move. The late nineteenth century saw Indian merchant and financial networks come alive again after centuries. Tamil Chettiar merchants and moneylenders spread across South East Asia, operating through a system of guild-like firms and agencies, usually run by members of the extended family. One of the largest of these firms, established by Muthiah Chetty in the early 1900s, was headquartered in Kanadukathan in Chettinad, Tamil Nadu, but with offices in Sri Lanka, Burma, Malaya and French Indo-China. Similarly, Gujarati traders and moneylenders established themselves along the coast from South Africa to Oman.

A significant concentration of Indians settled around Durban in South Africa. Some had come as indentured workers and stayed back while others came in search of economic opportunities. By the end of the nineteenth century, their numbers not only equalled that of the white population but they were also successfully competing with the Europeans as accountants, lawyers, clerks, traders and so on. This led to a series of discriminatory laws aimed at protecting the interests of the whites. This was the milieu to which a young lawyer called Mohandas K. Gandhi arrived in 1893. He was brought to South Africa by a well-established Gujarati businessman Dada Abdullah to assist in a personal matter. However, he was soon part of a movement to oppose anti-Indian laws. In 1894, the Natal Indian Congress was established with Gandhi as its secretary. Thus began a journey.

The Scramble for Africa

The nineteenth century was a tumultuous time for the African shores of the Indian Ocean. The Cape at the southern tip of Africa had long been a Dutch colony, but it was taken over by the British during the Napoleonic wars of the early 1800s. The treaty of 1814 confirmed British control, but a sizeable community of Dutch settlers continued to live there. Known as Afrikaners or Boers, they were very suspicious of the motives of their new rulers. When the British outlawed slavery, the Afrikaners saw it as a ruse to undermine them. So, from the 1830s, larger numbers of Boers took their families, livestock, guns and African slaves (now dubbed as servants), and moved into the interiors of the region.

Just as the Afrikaners were moving into the interiors of what is now South Africa, the area was also witnessing a large influx of Bantu tribes from the north-east. A prolonged drought in the early nineteenth century had caused these groups to migrate, but there was a more immediate cause—the rise of the Zulus. The Zulu tribe had been converted into a military machine by the famous leader Shaka. Using a combination of spears and fast-moving, disciplined units, the Zulus were even capable of taking on guns on occasion. As they expanded their territories, the other African tribes were forced to flee. This is known as the 'Mfecane' or The Scattering.

The current locations of various tribes in southern Africa is a direct outcome of this episode. Swaziland and Lesotho were both founded as a result of refugee groups banding together under powerful chiefs to defend themselves. The Xhosa (Nelson Mandela's tribe of origin) were among the worst affected as they were crushed between the Zulus and white settlers. Thus, the political dynamics of South Africa was never simple. There was just as much rivalry and bloodshed within each racial group as between them. The Khoi-San, the original inhabitants of the country, were the sorriest victims— already marginalized, enslaved and dispersed, they would play almost no role in subsequent events.

The next twist in the story was the discovery of diamond and gold deposits in South Africa. Until new deposits were found in Brazil during the eighteenth century, India had been the only source of diamonds in the world. The quantity and quality of South African diamonds, however, was at a different level altogether. This led to a mad rush. Within just a year of the first claims being made in 1867, 50,000 people were living in tents and other temporary shelters in Kimberley. By 1871, there were more people in Kimberley than in Cape Town! In that year alone, South Africa exported 2,69,000 carats of diamonds. With the boom came dubious claims, financial manipulation and large-scale gunrunning. It is estimated that 75,000 guns were sold in Kimberley between April 1873 and June 1874.

Eventually, order was restored and the entire operation at Kimberley was brought under the control of a single company: De Beers Consolidated Mines Limited. The man behind this consolidation was Cecil Rhodes. Rhodes had arrived in Kimberley as a dirt-poor teenager, but he had managed over time to establish himself as a formidable businessman and canny speculator. With the backing of wealthy financiers like the Rothschilds, he eventually came to control all the diamond mines of Kimberley. In 1890, he became the prime minister of Cape Colony. Rhodes now began to use his immense wealth and political power to push the interests of large mining magnates as well as expand the British Empire at the cost of both the Boers and the African tribes.

The frictions between the British and the Afrikaners eventually led to the Second Anglo-Boer War (1899–1902). The Boers made pre-emptive strikes and laid siege to a number of towns, including Kimberley. The British struck back with reinforcements shipped in from India. Indian soldiers would yet again play an important role in the course of events. Interestingly, Mohandas Gandhi also participated in the war by organizing a group of local Indian civilians into the Natal Indian Ambulance Corps that provided support to the British forces. By the middle of 1900, Boer resistance had begun to crumble and the British had taken over their capital, Pretoria.

The Boers now shifted to guerrilla tactics and continued to harass their adversaries. The British responded by creating large concentration camps to which the families of the Boer guerrillas were sent. At their height, the concentration camps held 1,12,000 inmates. Conditions in the camps were appalling and an estimated 28,000 Boers, mostly women and children, died over the course of a year from malnutrition and disease. Boer forces eventually surrendered in May 1902 and the two Boer republics were incorporated into the British Empire.

Cecil Rhodes did not live to see the end of the war as he died in March of that year. Rhodes lived during the high noon of British power and it would not have occurred to him that his beloved empire would cease to exist within half a century. It is somewhat ironic that I owe most of my education to Francis Xavier and Cecil Rhodes. I attended a high school named after the former and my years at Oxford were financed by a scholarship named after the latter. I am quite aware that in both cases I was not the intended beneficiary. This brings us to the tricky question of how to judge individuals from history—do we judge them by their intentions or by the consequences of their actions? Do we judge them only by the standards of their times or by some absolute yardstick? These are questions that scholars of history must constantly grapple with.

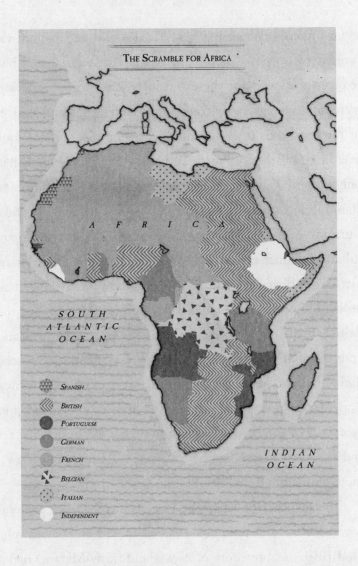

It is important to note that the British were not the only Europeans who occupied swathes of Africa in the late nineteenth century. In earlier times, Africa had been seen as an impediment on the way to Asia and occupation was limited to outposts along the coast. The Suez Canal had reduced the need for these outposts, but Africa's interiors were now seen as easily conquerable territories and sources of raw materials to feed industrial economies. France took over large swathes of North and West Africa. Germany had only become a united country in 1870, but it lost no time in claiming territories that we now know as Tanzania, Rwanda, Burundi, Namibia, Togo and Cameroon. When the Omani sultan of Zanzibar objected to the land grab in East Africa, Otto von Bismarck sent in his warships. The sultan had probably hoped that his British allies would help, but the British turned a blind eye and carried out their own land grab in what is now Kenya. A few years later, they placed their own candidate on the throne and effectively turned Zanzibar into a protectorate (i.e., it was controlled and protected by the British). Even tiny Belgium got into the act and occupied a large swathe of Central Africa, what is now the Democratic Republic of Congo.

The takeover of Africa had been so quick that colonial governments often struggled to keep up with it. For example, the British-held territory of Nyasaland (now Malawi) had a budget of just 10,000 pounds per year. This was just enough for ten European civilian officers, two military officers, seventy Sikh soldiers of the Punjab regiment and eighty-five porters from the Zanzibar coast. These were all the resources available to run a territory of 94,000 square kilometres with a population of one to two million.

National borders across the continent are still marked by the arbitrary straight lines drawn on a map by various European powers to mark out their acquisitions. These boundaries made no geographical or cultural sense on the ground, but this would not have bothered European colonizers who had convinced themselves that Africans had no history or culture. Denying a people's history and culture is an obvious way for a colonizing power to present everything preceding their arrival as the age of darkness and ignorance. Thus, the conquered territory can be termed as terra nullius or 'nobody's land', and the rights of the indigenous people can be denied. Indeed, the terra nullius argument was used in Australia till as recently as 1992 when the courts finally began to accept the land rights of the aborigines.

Not all the African tribes and kingdoms gave in without a fight, and in at least one instance the Europeans were beaten back. We have seen how the Ethiopians had preserved their independence in isolation for centuries despite being surrounded by the Arabs. Unfortunately, Ethiopia was one of the last independent territories left in Africa when the Italians too decided to join the scramble for Africa. In 1885, the Italians simply seized the port of Massawa on the

Red Sea and turned Ethiopia into a landlocked country. Emperor Menelik protested against this but found no support from major world powers. He was forced to sign a treaty that ceded Eritrea to Italy in return for recognizing his sovereignty over the highlands of the interior.

The Italians, however, had no intention of stopping with just the coast. They seized on some differences between the Italian and Amharic texts of the treaty and occupied northern Ethiopia. Menelik now began to smuggle in modern rifles and train an army. After a few initial skirmishes, the final battle took place at Adowa in March 1896. The Ethiopians inflicted a crushing defeat in which 3179 Italians and 2000 locally recruited auxiliaries were killed. Many more were wounded or taken prisoner. At this stage, Menelik may have been able to march on Eritrea, but he knew that his supply lines were stretched. Moreover, despite the victory, the Ethiopians were left with 7000 dead and over 10,000 wounded. So, the emperor accepted a new, more favourable treaty that explicitly recognized his independence.

Thus, Ethiopia would be the only African country to successfully defend itself against the colonial onslaught. The Italians had retained Eritrea but had been made to look very foolish. Mussolini would try to erase the memory of this defeat by invading and briefly occupying Ethiopia in the 1930s but would lose control of it during World War II.

Given their long history of defending their country against both the Arabs and the Europeans, often at great cost, the Ethiopians can be justly proud of their record of preserving their independence.

A Last-Ditch Attempt by the Dutch

When the twentieth century dawned, almost all of the shores of the Indian Ocean were already under European control. The British controlled the Indian subcontinent, Burma, Malaya, Australia and large sections of the East African coast. The French had established themselves in Indo-China (what is now Vietnam, Laos and Cambodia). Even a latecomer like Germany had managed to find a territory to colonize in East Africa and in the north-eastern quarter of New Guinea. But the Dutch, who had once been the dominant power, had steadily lost influence and territory. The British had taken away their former holdings in South Africa, Sri Lanka and Malaya. Although they had tightened control over their remaining territories in the Indonesian archipelago, the Dutch now decided to go further.

The small island of Bali was divided into a network of tiny kingdoms that, despite frequent Dutch interference, had remained effectively independent. In 1906, the Dutch used a minor pretext to land a large force on the island armed with modern rifles and machine guns. They knew that the Balinese were armed with no more than spears, shields and a few muskets. They also had a handful of small cannons that can still be viewed at the Bali Museum at Denpasar. They are beautifully decorated with dragon heads but are of an eighteenth-century design that would have been hopeless against modern weapons. In other words, both sides knew that the Balinese did not stand a chance.

The Dutch force landed on Sanur beach and faced little resistance as it marched inland. Along the way, it found that all settlements had been abandoned. Only when they approached the royal palace at Denpasar did they see signs of activity. There was no army to greet them, but they could see a lot of smoke rising and hear drums beating inside the palace compound. The invading force took up positions and waited. After a while, a ceremonial procession emerged from the main gate including the king, his queens and children, priests, servants and retainers. They all wore funerary garments and their finest jewellery. The women next walked up to the lined soldiers and mocked them, flinging their jewellery and gold coins at them.

Then a priest took out a kris, the traditional dagger, and stabbed the king to death in full view. This seems to have been the signal for the Balinese to pull out their krises and make a last charge. The Dutch machine guns and rifles mowed them all—men, women and children—down within minutes. There were soon mounds of dead bodies, probably numbering over a thousand. What the Dutch had just witnessed was the Balinese rite of puputan or 'the last stand' (similar to the Rajput practice of jauhar). This extraordinary event took place in the open field in front of what is now the Bali Museum in Denpasar. There is a memorial on the spot to commemorate it. The nearby museum has a few photographs that show the aftermath of the massacre.

The Dutch commanders, however, only waited to allow the soldiers to collect all the jewellery and loot the palace before setting it on fire. They then marched to the next kingdom where they witnessed a similar sequence of events. They finally left after forcing the king of Klungkung, the senior most of Bali's rulers, to sign a humiliating treaty. Not surprisingly, the Balinese were seething with anger that would spill over into riots. This gave the Dutch the pretext to return in 1908 and attack Klungkung. Yet again, the Balinese opted to commit puputan. The king charged out wielding his kris along with 200 of his followers and they were all shot dead. His six queens committed ritual suicide; the palace was looted and razed to the ground.

When reports of the events in Bali finally reached Europe, they caused uproar. It did not help that the invaders had themselves photographed the atrocities. By now the supposed civilizing mission of the European colonial enterprise was sounding increasingly hollow. The incidents in Bali were merely the last nails in the coffin. Within a few years, the barbarity of the First World War would take away even the pretence of moral and civilizational superiority.

CHAPTER 10

FROM DUSK TO A NEW DAWN

As we have seen, the Indian Ocean rim was dominated by various European powers at the beginning of the twentieth century. With the loss of many of their colonies in the Americas, the Europeans had greater control over the Indian Ocean than over the Atlantic. It had taken centuries of war and colonization to create this state of affairs, and not many would have imagined that it would all change drastically within a few decades.

Then came the First World War.

The Exploits of the Emden

While much of the action of World War I took place in the trenches of Europe and around the Mediterranean, the Indian Ocean rim also saw a number of important engagements. One fascinating episode relates to the German light cruiser *Emden*. When the war began in July 1914, the *Emden* was one of a handful of German vessels that found themselves stranded on the other side of the world at Tsingtao (Qingdao), a German-controlled enclave along the Chinese coast. It soon became clear that Tsingtao and other German colonies in the East were not defensible and the ships would have to return home via the Pacific Ocean.

THE EMDEN

However, Karl von Muller, the commander of the *Emden*, asked for permission to head west to the Indian Ocean. Permission was granted and the *Emden* slipped through neutral Dutch-controlled waters into the Indian Ocean. Muller added a fake smoke funnel in order to disguise his ship as a British cruiser. By early September, the *Emden* was in the Bay of Bengal where it began to systematically attack and sink ships belonging to the British and their allies. No one knew what was happening, and this caused a panic. British intelligence had been under the impression that the *Emden* was in the Pacific along with the rest of the German fleet. Karl von Muller had earned a reputation as a gentleman privateer because he minimized casualties, treated his prisoners well and let them go at the first opportunity. It was only through information gleaned from some released crews that the authorities in Calcutta realized what was happening.

On 22 September, the *Emden* unexpectedly appeared off the coast of Madras and proceeded to bombard the port. The raid lasted for barely half an hour, but the 125-odd shells set ablaze oil containers and threw the city into chaos. The ship then disappeared as suddenly as it had appeared. Although the damage was limited, the raid had a major psychological impact on the city and for a generation the word 'emden' would be used as Tamil slang to denote maverick cunning or resourcefulness. There is a plaque commemorating it along the eastern wall of the High Court. It marks the spot where one of the shells landed.

The *Emden* now sailed down the coast towards Sri Lanka, capturing and sinking more ships along the way. Eventually, it headed for Diego Garcia, a remote British-held island in the southern Indian Ocean. Muller was pleasantly surprised to find that the islanders had not heard about the war, since modern communications technology had not yet connected every point on the planet. The *Emden* was, therefore, able to carry out repairs and refuel in peace. At this stage, Muller could have decided to head home around the Cape or make for an Ottoman-held port on the Red Sea, but he opted for his most audacious raid yet—an attack on Penang in the Malacca Straits.

The *Emden* slipped into Penang harbour at dawn on 28 October using the extra funnel to disguise itself. It soon spotted an old Russian cruiser that had stopped for repairs. The *Emden* opened fire before the Russians could respond and destroyed the ship. The *Emden* was then engaged by a number of British and French ships but managed to fight its way out, sinking a French destroyer along the way. The Penang raid added to Muller's legend and was a big blow to the prestige of the Allies. Not only had a German ship made its way into the Malacca Straits, but it had also single-handedly caused a lot of damage before getting away. Now, every warship in the Indian Ocean was pressed into looking for the *Emden*.

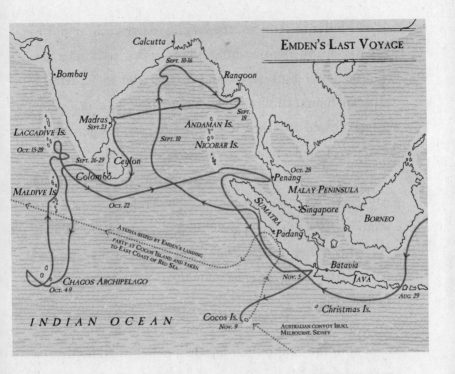

EMDEN'S LAST VOYAGE

Muller now headed for the Cocos Islands, south of Sumatra. The Allies had a major wireless and cable communications station on one of the islands. The Germans planned to knock out the communications hub and a small party was sent ashore to destroy the equipment. Here, Muller's luck finally ran out. One of the operators on the island was able to send out an SOS message and alert an Australian naval convoy that happened to be nearby. The convoy included a state-of-the-art cruiser HMAS *Sydney* that could outmatch the *Emden* for firepower. The sudden appearance of *Sydney* forced Muller to abandon the landing party and sail out to meet the enemy. The two cruisers bombarded each other, but the *Sydney* was both faster and had heavier guns. After a couple of hours, Muller realized that his ship was sinking and was forced to beach it in order to save the remaining crew. Sometime later, he surrendered.

There is a bit more to the story. The German landing party that had been abandoned by Muller managed to commandeer a schooner and sailed all the way to Yemen, from where they fought their way to Turkish-controlled territory. The Turks arranged for them to travel by rail to Istanbul, where they told their remarkable story. Meanwhile, Karl von Muller was taken as a prisoner of war and held in Malta until the end of the war, when he returned home to a hero's welcome. Most of the remaining crew were imprisoned in Singapore.

The Flapping of a Butterfly's Wings

Indian soldiers played a pivotal role in the building of the British Empire, but colonial authorities were always worried that the soldiers would switch loyalties. Under normal circumstances, all colonial powers maintained a sizeable force of European regiments in the colonies as backup, but WWI had forced the withdrawal of many of these units. The balance worsened as the British began to recruit Indian soldiers on a large scale to fight in the war. Approximately 1.3 million Indian soldiers and auxiliaries participated in the war, of which around 74,000 lost their lives. Indian soldiers stopped the German advance at Ypres, and thousands died in the trenches of Europe and at Gallipoli. Even less remembered are the battles they fought in the Indian Ocean rim.

One of the first places where Indian soldiers were deployed was in German East Africa (now Tanzania) where they campaigned against the spirited guerrilla tactics of Paul von Lettow-Vorbeck. Despite being cut off from supplies and reinforcements, and with British Indian troops in hot pursuit, the wily Lettow-Vorbeck and his men would keep up German resistance in Africa till the end of the war. Recognizing the importance of India as a source for troops and supplies, the Germans and the Turks were very keen to provoke a revolt. One strategy was to instigate the Muslim population across the Middle East and the subcontinent to rise up against the British.

The Ottoman sultan's supposed position as the caliph of all Muslims was played up. A German agent called Wilhelm Wassmuss sent to instigate the tribes of southern Iran to attack British interests in the region. He even spread rumours that the German kaiser had converted to Islam and adopted the name 'Haji Wilhelm Mohammad'! Wassmuss told the tribes that a grand Turko-German army would soon march through Iran into India and throw out the British infidels. Reports soon began to reach Quetta that a powerful Baloch chief was already in touch with the Germans. British intelligence took this threat seriously and an expeditionary force was sent out from India to Iraq in order to pre-empt the possible invasion. They would simultaneously use their own agent, T.E. Lawrence, better known as 'Lawrence of Arabia', to instigate the Arabs against the Turks.

The British Indian troops led by Major General Townshend initially won a series of easy victories in Iraq as they made their way inland. However, as they closed in on Baghdad in November 1915, the Turks put up an unexpectedly fierce resistance at Ctesiphon (once the capital of the pre-Islamic Persian Empire). Townshend was forced to retreat to the town of Kut to wait for reinforcements. Meanwhile, the Turks surrounded the town and enforced a siege. With the evacuation of Gallipoli, the Allies suddenly found themselves in a difficult situation, and the Turks were able to fend off British relief columns that had got bogged down by floods on the Tigris. The siege of Kut would last five agonizing months till the starving garrison finally surrendered on 29 April 1916.

The Turkish leader Enver Pasha celebrated the victory by declaring himself a Ghazi (Holy Warrior). Around 3000 British and 6000 Indian troops were captured and force-marched to Turkey as prisoners. Although Townshend was treated quite well in captivity, many of his men died from disease and ill-treatment. The Haider Pasha cemetery in Istanbul contains the graves and ashes of a few of these soldiers. Few Indians today remember these men and their deaths in faraway lands. Similarly, the city of Mumbai has a memorial to Indian sailors who died in WWI. It is tucked away in a sailors' hostel in the old port area and almost no one visits it.

The events at Gallipoli and Kut had resurrected the reputation and morale of the Turkish military. The British now needed a decisive victory and a formidable force of 1,50,000 men was assembled. These men were put under the command of Sir Stanley Maude, one of the most experienced generals in the British Empire. In early 1917, this huge army pushed towards Baghdad against determined Turkish resistance. But on the night of 10 March, the British saw a bright glow over the city of Baghdad: the Turks were burning everything of value before retreating. By noon the next day, General Maude's troops had occupied the shattered ruins—almost all major government buildings had been burnt down, shops and homes had been looted, rotting corpses lay everywhere.

The fall of Baghdad also meant that the German agent Wassmuss found himself isolated in southern Iran. Few tribesmen now believed his story of a grand Turko-German army marching to India. However, his greatest failure was not his fading ability to rouse the Tangistani tribesmen but a small error that had major consequences for the German war effort. During his adventures in southern Iran, Wassmuss had been captured on one occasion by a pro-British tribe. Although he made a daring escape, he was forced to leave behind his belongings, which included the German diplomatic codebook. This codebook eventually made its way to 'Room 40'—the specialist code-breaking unit in London. Armed with Wassmuss's codebook, the cryptographers uncovered a German plan to unleash all-out submarine warfare against the Allies while simultaneously bringing Mexico and Japan into the war. The Germans had promised the Mexicans that if they entered the war, they would be helped to recover Arizona, Texas and New Mexico from the United States. The British gleefully passed this information to the Americans. On 1 March 1917, newspaper headlines across the United States revealed the story to an outraged American public. The sinking of American merchant ships by U-boats over the next few weeks made it clear that the United States could no longer remain neutral. On 6 April, President Wilson declared war on Germany. The fate of the

Central Powers was now sealed. Thus, a small mistake by a secret agent in the Persian Gulf had a big influence on the course of world history; the flapping of a butterfly's wings had caused a hurricane.

Revolutionaries and Conspiracies

Many senior leaders of the Indian National Congress, including Mahatma Gandhi, supported the British during the First World War with the expectation that this would be rewarded with major political concessions after the war. But other Indians, revolutionaries who believed in using armed rebellion to defeat the British, thought that the war presented an opportunity to weaken British rule. These revolutionaries played a very important role in how events unfolded.

Punjab and Bengal were the two main hubs of the revolutionary movement, although there were several others scattered across the country, most notably Varanasi. The movement was initially made up of a number of groups working in isolation, but they were already beginning to communicate with each other before the war began due to the efforts of Rash Behari Bose and his young lieutenant Sachindra Nath Sanyal. They were also in touch with like-minded activists among expatriate Indians scattered around the world. One of them was Har Dayal who was studying at St John's College, Oxford.

While in England, Har Dayal was influenced by the ideas of Vinayak Damodar 'Veer' Savarkar, a revolutionary then operating out of India House in London. Savarkar was arrested in 1910 and, despite a dramatic escape attempt in Marseilles, was sent to prison in Port Blair in the Andamans. Har Dayal then shifted to California, where he continued to organize support for revolutionary activities among newly arrived Indian students and immigrants, especially Sikhs from Punjab. In other words, an elaborate revolutionary network was already in place before war was declared. Indeed, the revolutionaries had nearly managed to kill Lord Hardinge, the viceroy, in December 1912 while he rode on a ceremonial elephant through Delhi's Chandni Chowk. The viceroy sustained severe injuries from the bomb but survived; some of the attackers were caught, but the main planner, Rash Behari Bose, escaped.

When war was declared and it became clear that the British would have to rely heavily on Indian troops, the revolutionaries immediately came up with a plan to take advantage of the situation by instigating a coordinated revolt by Indian regiments. Rash Behari Bose and Sachindra Nath Sanyal coordinated between large numbers of clandestine participants—Sikhs returning from North America, revolutionaries in Bengal and regiments were primed for mutiny from Punjab to Burma. The date of what would be known as the Ghadar uprising was set for 21 February 1915.

Unfortunately, the uprising went awry before it began. It had been planned that the sequence of events would be triggered when the regiments in Mian Mir, on the north-west frontier, and Punjab first rose in revolt. However, just five days before the revolt, an informer called Kirpal Singh revealed the plans to the colonial authorities in Lahore. Learning of this, Bose decided to bring the date forward, to 19 February, in order to deny the authorities time to react but British intelligence was already on full alert. Police raids captured several of the conspirators, and Indian guards at all armouries were replaced by British ones. The element of surprise had been totally lost. In the face of such decisive action, the soldiers lost their nerve and momentum simply melted away.

The only place that saw a full-scale revolt was Singapore where predominantly Muslim regiments mutinied on 15 February and took over large parts of the island. They also freed the Germans captured from the *Emden* and asked them to join the battle but were refused. It took the authorities a full week of fighting, backed by reinforcements, to quell the uprising. Dozens of mutineers would be lined up against a wall on Outram Street and publicly executed by a firing squad. With his plans unravelling and the authorities closing in, Bose first sought refuge in the narrow lanes of Varanasi where the Sanyal family could use its network of family and friends to temporarily hide a fugitive. However, as police raids mounted, he decided to escape to Japan where he would keep up his efforts for the next three decades.

Sachin Sanyal stayed behind to organize the remaining revolutionaries. They received a morale boost when they heard that the German war machine had decided to back them. A body called the Indian Revolutionary Committee was set up in Berlin and was given full embassy status. Since the United States was still neutral at this stage, the German embassy in Washington DC acquired 30,000 rifles and pistols (plus ammunition) and began to secretly arrange for them to be sent to India. Two vessels—a schooner called *Annie Larsen* and a tanker called *Maverick*—were hired to take the weapons across the Pacific to Asia where they would be divided into smaller vessels to be carried to India. The idea was that well-armed revolutionaries would capture Calcutta on Christmas Day, 1915. Again, things did not go according to plan. The two ships failed to make their rendezvous on the agreed date and location. Worse, a German agent named Vincent Kraft was arrested in Singapore; he agreed to divulge information in exchange for a large sum of money and being allowed to emigrate to the US under a new identity.

Boats carrying weapons to India through Thailand and the Bay of Bengal were intercepted. Finally, in a series of lightning raids, 300 conspirators were arrested in Calcutta and Burma. The Christmas Day plot had been foiled.

As one can see, the Ghadar uprising and the Christmas Day plot were very large-scale plans to overthrow British colonial rule in India. Although they failed, they had both come closer to being executed than most people know. However, the dynamics set in motion by the revolutionaries would influence events in the Second World War and eventually contribute to India gaining freedom in 1947.

The Prison across the Water

By early 1916, a large number of Indian revolutionaries had been captured. Several were hanged, while others were given long prison sentences, including Sachindra Nath Sanyal, who was sentenced to life imprisonment in the dreaded Cellular Jail in Port Blair. This prison complex in the Andaman Islands was where hardened criminals as well as political prisoners were sent. It was known in India as 'Kala Pani' or the Black Waters. The Andaman and Nicobar Islands are a string of Indian islands in the Bay of Bengal. Although separated from the mainland by a large body of water, people had been living here for a very long time. Given their location close to major maritime trade routes, it is not surprising that the islands were known to ancient and medieval mariners and are mentioned in several old texts.

CELLULAR JAIL
'KALA PANI'

In the eighteenth century, the Danes, of all people, came to control these islands, but they failed to establish an economically viable settlement. Eventually, they handed the islands over to the British, who decided to use it as a penal colony and built the Cellular Jail complex there. Barindra Ghosh, younger brother of the famous spiritual leader Sri Aurobindo, was sent there in 1909 for his revolutionary activities. He would spend over a decade there and has left us vivid and surprisingly humorous descriptions of life in the prison. Ghosh tells us that prisoners were made to do hard physical labour—making coir ropes, turning the oil press and so on. He also says that the prisoners, especially the revolutionaries, were constantly subjected to mental and physical torture in an attempt to systematically break the will of the revolutionaries.

Mahatma Gandhi and the Indian National Congress had expected major concessions after the war, but they soon realized that Indians would get little in return for their cooperation. Instead, the British introduced the draconian Rowlatt Act in 1919. This gave the authorities sweeping powers to arrest and detain activists. It was the colonial government's response to fears that the returning Indian soldiers would be susceptible to revolutionary ideas. The law elicited strong protests and, amidst the deteriorating political climate, culminated in the Jallianwala Bagh massacre in April 1919. Like the massacre perpetrated by the Dutch in Bali, the cold-blooded murder of so many unarmed men, women and children ended British claims of civilizational superiority.

The colonial government tried to retrieve the situation by giving a general amnesty to several of the revolutionaries including Sachindra Nath Sanyal. The released revolutionaries now agreed to work with Mahatma Gandhi on a movement of non-violent non-cooperation. The protests spread very quickly and brought the subcontinent to a standstill.

It looked like the British authorities had finally been cornered but, just as some form of victory seemed imminent, Gandhi unilaterally suspended the movement after a mob in Chauri-Chaura set fire to a police station and killed several policemen. Gandhi argued that this incident had violated the principle of non-violence, and it created a rift between him and the revolutionaries.

Sachin Sanyal now reverted to organizing the various revolutionary groups under an umbrella organization called the Hindustan Republican Association in 1924 and under it began to build the Hindustan Republican Army. It was during this period that Sachin Sanyal came into contact with a young, rising star in the Congress party— Subhash Chandra Bose, later to be known simply as 'Netaji' (literally, the Leader). Sanyal would be sent back to prison a few years later and many of his followers would be killed or executed, but Subhash Bose would leverage the international networks pioneered by the revolutionaries in his attempt to build an armed revolt against the British during the Second World War.

The Fall of Singapore

Hollywood films may have led us to believe that the attack on Pearl Harbour marked Japan's entry into the Second

World War. In reality, the very first shots were fired at 10.20 p.m. on 7 December 1941 on the beaches of Kota Bharu on the north-eastern corner of the Malay Peninsula. Despite resistance from Indian troops in the area, the Japanese were soon storming the beaches and landing men and equipment. By 4.30 a.m., Japanese bombers were making raids on Singapore. British commanders in Malaya had anticipated the possibility of such an attack but had thinly spread their troops as they did not know exactly where the landing would take place. Moreover, the best Indian regiments had already been deployed on the other side of the Indian Ocean in Africa. The Allied troops in Malaya were inexperienced new recruits from India and Australia who, in many cases, had not completed their basic training. What made it worse was they were backed neither from the air nor from the sea.

Soon the Japanese were landing troops at will and making their way down the peninsula. The defence crumbled so quickly that in many areas the invading force cycled over long distances without encountering serious resistance. When British Prime Minister Churchill realized what was happening, he ordered that Singapore should be defended to the last. He also ordered the cruiser HMS *Repulse* and the battleship HMS *Prince of Wales* to sail to Singapore. Their arrival in Singapore on 2 December brought some cheer to the defenders, but military strategists should have realized that they were sitting ducks without air cover. By 10 December, both the ships had been sunk by torpedo bombers. Recognizing the deteriorating situation, Lieutenant General Arthur Percival ordered his remaining troops to fall back on Singapore.

Despite the dire situation, there was still a sense of confidence that Singapore would hold. Even as the Japanese were closing in on the island in mid-January 1942, Robinson's department store was still advertising 'Snappy American Frocks for day and afternoon wear $12.50' and the Raffles Hotel was still organizing dances. By the first week of February, however, the Japanese had taken over Johor and were bombarding the island from the air and by artillery. There is an oft-repeated legend that Singapore's big guns pointed south towards the sea in anticipation of a naval assault and could not be turned around against attackers from the north. This is not entirely accurate. The problem was that they were supplied with armour-piercing ammunition meant to be used against ships and were not effective against infantry. Percival now had to guess where Japanese commander Tomoyuki Yamashita would make his main assault. Eventually, he decided to place his best troops to the north-east.

This proved to be a big mistake, as the main Japanese landing took place from the north-west where the Johor

Strait is at its narrowest. Overcoming resistance from Australian units defending this sector, the Japanese were soon closing in on the city. On 13 February, the 1st Malay Regiment attempted a last desperate defence of Pasir Panjang ridge. By this point, the centre of the city, including the underground command centre at Fort Canning, was being pounded constantly and civilian casualties were mounting. The situation was clearly hopeless. On 15 February, Percival drove to the Ford Motor factory in Bukit Timah to personally discuss the terms of surrender with Yamashita. It says something of the desperate situation that Percival had to borrow a car from the Bata Shoe Company in order to go for his meeting. Thus began the Japanese occupation of Singapore. For the Chinese population, in particular, this would be a period of extreme hardship.

Netaji and the Indian National Army

When the Second World War broke out in 1939, the British again looked to India for troops and support; some 2.5 million Indians would participate in the Allied war effort. However, having learnt from the experience of the previous war, Mahatma Gandhi and the Indian National Congress decided not to cooperate with the colonial government and launched the non-violent Quit India movement. Not all

Indian leaders agreed with the decision to launch the Quit India movement as they felt that opposition to fascism was the greater cause. Still others felt that the war had produced a second golden opportunity to throw off colonial rule through armed revolt. By this time, the senior revolutionary leaders from the previous war had mostly been killed or were in prison, so it fell on 'Netaji' Subhash Bose to take up this cause.

Bose had drifted away from the Congress, but the British still considered him a dangerous leader and had placed him under house arrest in Calcutta. In early 1941, he made a dramatic escape and made his way in disguise through Afghanistan and the Soviet Union to Germany where he requested help from the Nazi government. He was treated well and given a patient hearing, but he soon realized that the Germans were unwilling or unable to commit large resources to his cause. While Bose was wondering about his next move, he received news of the fall of Singapore. Soon, he heard that veteran revolutionary Rash Behari Bose was organizing surrendered Indian soldiers into the Indian National Army (INA) that would fight alongside the Japanese (recall that Rash Behari had escaped to Japan in 1915 after the collapse of the Ghadar uprising).

Netaji next travelled by submarine to Singapore where the older Bose handed him the command of the INA on

4 July 1943. The handover ceremony took place at the Cathay Cinema theatre where Netaji delivered a rousing speech. The next day, he reviewed the INA troops at the Padang grounds in the middle of the city. Of the 40,000 Indians who had surrendered in Singapore, the majority opted for the INA. Meanwhile, the Japanese had taken over the Andaman and Nicobar Islands and handed de jure control to Netaji. This would be the only piece of Indian territory that the Provisional Government would ever control. The INA now joined the Japanese on their march through Burma to the eastern gates of India.

SUBHASH CHANDRA BOSE
AND THE INA

The British responded by rushing a large number of troops to defend the line. Through the summer of 1944, the two sides simultaneously fought ferocious battles in Kohima (now capital of the state of Nagaland) and in Imphal (capital of Manipur). These are considered among the most hard-fought battles of the Second World War. The Japanese lost and the tide of war turned in favour of the Allies. The campaign would cost the Japanese side 53,000 in dead or missing while the Allies lost 16,500. From an Indian perspective, the tragedy of these battles was that Indian soldiers fought and died bravely on both sides, sacrificing their lives for someone else's empires. Even worse was the famine that killed 3 million people in Bengal in 1943. Crop failure and the disruption of rice supplies from Burma may have initially triggered the problem, but the British colonial government did little to provide relief. Instead, they commandeered all the boats in order to deny the invading army the means to traverse the riverine terrain. This meant that locals could not even fish.

We know now that the British prime minister, Winston Churchill, was fully aware of the dire situation but seems to have deliberately delayed and diverted supplies as part of a scorched earth strategy against the advancing Japanese. He is reported to have remarked that Indians were a 'beastly people with a beastly religion' and that the famine was caused by Bengalis who 'bred like rabbits'. As the Japanese retreated, the INA fought against the Allied advance in Burma but by early 1945, it had effectively disintegrated. A day after Japan surrendered on 15 August, Subhash Bose flew from

Singapore to Taiwan. What happened next is a mystery. The official line is that he died in a plane crash in Taiwan, but the story was disputed right from the start. It remains a highly controversial matter to this day.

Bose's decision to ask Axis powers for help also remains controversial. After all, from the Jallianwala massacre to the Bengal famine, when viewed from an Indian perspective, there was little to morally distinguish the Allies from the Axis powers. They were just two sets of evil empires and Bose was merely using every available opportunity to free his enslaved people. Besides, he was using the very same international support networks established by revolutionaries like Sachin Sanyal and Rash Behari Bose a generation earlier. Netaji's actions and the formation of the INA are thus part of the longer history of the revolutionary movement and its long-standing connections with Germany and Japan.

The Decisive Rebellion

From the Ghadar plot to the INA, the revolutionaries had made several unsuccessful attempts to incite a revolt among Indian troops on whom the British Empire relied. Their efforts eventually did bear fruit. The general public had been largely unaware of the activities of the INA due to wartime censorship, but it caused a sensation when the prisoners of war were brought back and put on trial. As their stories circulated among the troops, rumblings of discontent began to grow. These culminated in the Royal Indian Navy mutiny of 18–23 February 1946.

The episode was triggered by a minor altercation in Bombay over the quality of food being served to sailors but, given the overall mood, it quickly became a full-fledged revolt. The sailors stopped obeying their officers and took control of a number of ships and shore establishments. The sailors were not novices: this was just a few months after the war, so the British were dealing with battle-hardened veterans. Soon, they had taken over the wireless communications sets on their ships and were coordinating their actions. As the news spread, students, industrial workers and others went on strike and marched in support of the mutineers. Sailors in Calcutta and Karachi also mutinied; at its height, the unrest involved seventy-eight ships, twenty shore establishments and 20,000 sailors. When Baloch and Gurkha troops in Karachi were sent in to quell the revolt, they flatly refused to open fire on the sailors. Officers and pilots of the Royal Indian Air Force similarly refused to help the authorities.

Unfortunately for the mutineers, they received no support from the Indian political leadership of the time. Both the Indian National Congress and the Muslim League asked them to surrender. Subhash Bose was missing, and the senior revolutionary leaders who had tried so hard to trigger exactly such a mutiny were no longer alive. Lacking political leadership, the sailors eventually surrendered. Despite various assurances, large numbers of sailors were court-martialled and dismissed. Although the episode ended peacefully, the British colonial administration must have realized that they were rapidly losing control over their Indian soldiers. Just a week after the naval mutiny, the signals unit of the army in Jabalpur also rebelled. It was quite clear that another large-scale revolt was only a matter of time. Once the loyalty of members of the Indian armed forces had been undermined, the British Empire began to unwind not just in the Indian subcontinent but worldwide. The revolutionaries had finally succeeded.

The Majapahit Dream

The Dutch had simply crumbled without much resistance when the Japanese invaded their colonies in the East Indies. For their own interests, the Japanese had in turn encouraged a number of nationalists like Sukarno during their occupation. So, two days after Japan surrendered, the Indonesian leaders made a proclamation of independence. There were a number of groups that had emerged in the political vacuum, including Islamists and Communists, but Sukarno's Republicans were the strongest. The problem was that the Dutch intended to return and reclaim their colonies. However, they did not have the resources at the time to reoccupy the islands, so they asked the British for help. The British landed a large contingent of Indian troops near Surabaya; there was heavy fighting and the British commander, General Mallaby, was assassinated. The Indonesians were eventually pushed out, but there had been significant casualties on both sides. The episode further added to growing dissatisfaction among the Indian troops, who did not see why they should risk their lives for such a cause. Some of them switched sides. As the unrest continued to spread across the islands, the Allies were forced to deploy surrendered Japanese troops in order to maintain control.

An important factor that bolstered the Indonesian resolve was that events seemed to be playing out an ancient prophecy. The twelfth century Javanese king Jayabaya is said to have prophesied that three centuries of rule by white men would end with the coming of short yellow men who would leave after just one harvest. Other than the minor discrepancy that the Japanese had stayed for three harvests, the prophecy seemed to be coming true. In early 1946, the Dutch began to land thousands of troops on Bali backed by support from the air. They faced fierce resistance from a small guerrilla force organized hurriedly by Ngurah Rai. The guerrillas were eventually cornered and Ngurah Rai ordered the puputan. Yet again, the Balinese fought to the last man. The international airport in Bali is named after the guerrilla leader who was killed during the last stand.

Subsequently, the Dutch managed to take over many of the main towns with the support of Allied troops, but the Republicans continued to control the countryside. Realizing that the Republicans were too well entrenched to be wished away, the Dutch finally accepted the Linggadjati Agreement on 15 November 1946, which gave the Republicans authority over the islands of Sumatra, Java and Madura. The two sides also agreed to work towards the establishment of the United States of Indonesia. Unfortunately, the Dutch were merely buying time in order to organize themselves. In May 1947, their troops occupied large parts of Java and Sumatra and pushed the Republican forces into small enclaves. The country descended into war. An attempt by the United States to force a compromise failed.

Amidst the chaos, a daredevil pilot from Odisha called Biju Patnaik flew secret missions into Java and rescued two key Indonesian rebel leaders (he would later go on to become the chief minister of Odisha). Prime Minister Nehru, meanwhile, organized the Asian Conference in

New Delhi, which then pressured the UN Security Council to take action against the Dutch. It is remarkable that the first foreign policy action taken by newly independent India was to support Indonesia's freedom movement, as if an ancient civilizational kinship had been suddenly rekindled. It was also appropriate that someone from Kalinga had played an important role in the sequence of events. It is even said that Sukarno named his daughter Megawati, meaning 'Goddess of the Clouds' in Sanskrit, in honour of Biju Patnaik's heroics in the sky.

The UN had forced a ceasefire, but the Dutch were still not prepared to leave. They tried to instigate different parts of the archipelago against the Republicans using the bogey of Javan domination. Finally, the United States threatened the Dutch with cutting off the Marshall Plan aid and forced them to accept a provisional government with Sukarno as president and Mohammad Hatta as prime minister on 27 December 1949. Sukarno would spend the next decade securing the territorial claims of his fledgling country against secessionists, communist rebels and the continued interference of the Dutch. It is said that he was driven by a vision of re-establishing the Majapahit Empire and that a map of the medieval empire hung in his office—an example of how current events are often influenced by civilizational memories.

The End of an Era

Once India gained independence in 1947, the whole colonial project in the Indian Ocean began to unravel. One by one, all the countries in the region began to demand independence and the Europeans were soon reduced to fighting a rearguard action. Their reduced status was clearly demonstrated by the Suez Crisis of 1956. The sequence of events was triggered by Egyptian leader Gamal Abdel Nasser who nationalized the Suez Canal Company. The British, with support from the French and the Israelis, invaded Egypt in order to take control of the canal. Although the invaders succeeded militarily, they faced severe criticism from the United States and the Soviet Union and were forced to withdraw meekly. The episode can be said to mark the end of Britain's reign as a world power.

Within the next fifteen years, the British and other colonial powers would free virtually all their colonies in the Indian Ocean rim. The withdrawal was far from peaceful and involved many conflicts, including anti-communist operations in Malaya and the Mau Mau uprising in Kenya. Tens of thousands of Europeans went back 'home', including those who had been born in the colonies, as well as many of mixed parentage. Nevertheless, there were exceptions. In South Africa and Rhodesia (now Zimbabwe), a dominant white minority was strong enough to remain in power for several years after the departure of colonial backing. In Australia, of course, those of European origin had replaced the indigenous population as the majority.

Perhaps the most determined attempt to retain colonial possessions was made by the French in Vietnam. In the political vacuum left by Japan's surrender, the Viet Minh led by Ho Chi Minh had taken over Hanoi and declared independence. Nonetheless, the country was occupied by Allied troops—the British in the south and Chinese in the north—and the French were soon given back control of the administration. The French made several promises about granting freedom, but it became apparent that they had no intention of leaving. Things dragged on till 1954 when the French assembled a large military force, backed from the air, in order to expel the Viet Minh from the north of the country. However, the Vietnamese outwitted and trapped the colonial army in the Battle of Dien Bien Phu and inflicted a devastating defeat. After this, the French departed. The north of the country was in the hands of Ho Chi Minh while the south was under a puppet regime backed by the Americans.

The departure of the Europeans unfortunately did not mean that the Indian Ocean rim became a postcolonial utopia. The Vietnam War would consume the country till North Vietnamese tanks finally crashed through the gates of the presidential palace in Saigon in April 1975. In Cambodia, almost two million people were killed by the Khmer Rouge regime between 1975 and 1978 in a brutal attempt to create a communist agrarian paradise. In East Pakistan, the West Pakistani army perpetrated a genocide that killed as many as three million Bengalis and pushed ten million refugees into India. This resulted in the Indo-Pak War of 1971 and the creation of Bangladesh. In the western Indian Ocean, Ethiopia and Eritrea fought a long, bitter war that only ended in 1991. Yemen was locked in a civil war between the north and the south. The Solomonic dynasty in Ethiopia had outlived the Arab and the European expansionism, but it did not survive the social forces unleashed by modernity. An ageing Haile Selassie was removed from the throne in a military coup in 1974. A few years later, the Iranian revolution would bring about the fall of Mohammad Reza Pahlavi, the last shah of Iran.

The unwinding of the European empires also disrupted the commercial and human networks that had been created over years. For instance, there were over a million Indians in Burma, accounting for more than half the population of Rangoon in the 1930s. After the military coup in 1962, their businesses were forcibly nationalized and large numbers were expelled. Similarly, Idi Amin gave Indians in Uganda ninety days to pack up and leave in 1972. Some went back to India but many went to the United Kingdom, where they would rebuild their lives. Under French rule, Saigon too had been home to a significant number of Indians. They were not expelled, but as economic conditions deteriorated during the war, they gradually drifted away.

The Spectacular Rise of Singapore

The first subregion in the Indian Ocean rim to witness rapid economic change was the Persian Gulf. Commercially viable oil was first discovered in Masjid-e-Suleiman, Iran, in 1908. Bahrain was producing oil by 1932 followed by Dammam in Saudi Arabia and Kuwait by 1938. By the 1970s, the wealth accumulated from oil exports had transformed the economic and social fabric of the region. The boom sucked in construction workers, engineers, clerks, corporate managers, nurses, teachers and other service providers from the rest of the world, particularly the Indian subcontinent. The small port of Dubai, once known for the pearl trade, did not have much oil, but it positioned itself as the key commercial hub in the region and evolved over decades into the glitzy city we see today. In contrast to the oil-driven success of the Gulf states, the most remarkable economic transformation in the Indian Ocean rim was arguably achieved by a tiny, crowded island with so few natural resources that it even had to import water: Singapore.

In 1963, the British colonies of Singapore, Sarawak and North Borneo (Sabah) agreed to enter into a federation with the states of the Malay Peninsula in order to form Malaysia. The main objection to this came from Indonesia's Sukarno, who saw it as a 'neocolonial plot' to thwart his plan of rebuilding the Majapahit Empire. Trouble began to brew soon afterwards, as the Peoples' Action Party (PAP), led by a firebrand socialist called Lee Kuan Yew, began to be viewed with suspicion by Malay politicians. They worried that he would leverage his base in Singapore to gain inroads into Sabah, Sarawak and the Chinese population in the peninsula. Matters were further complicated by widespread race riots in Singapore that killed twenty-three people. Malay politicians soon decided to squeeze Singapore out of the federation and, on the morning of 9 August 1965, the city state's proclamation of independence was announced over the radio. Later that day, Lee Kuan Yew broke down in tears at an emotional press conference.

The future of the tiny, slum-ridden island looked grim. The British added to the prognosis by announcing that they would be shutting down their military base—they no longer had an empire and had no need to control the Malacca Straits. Lee Kuan Yew, now prime minister, knew that he

SINGAPORE, THEN AND NOW

needed to quickly find a new economic engine for his city state. He decided to ask multinational companies to set up their manufacturing hub in Singapore by offering them rule of law, ease of doing business and low taxes. This was not only a break from his early socialist rhetoric but was also very different from what other newly independent countries were doing at that time (and much more in tune with the ideals of Stamford Raffles). Foreign capital financed capacities in sectors ranging from ready-made garments to oil refining. The Singaporeans also used the naval facilities abandoned by the British to build out a shipbuilding and repair cluster. The economic strategy was very successful.

In the 1980s, the government decided that the economy needed to be diversified and upgraded, and brought in new industries like electronics and pharmaceuticals. It also invested in top-quality infrastructure and public housing. All of this turned Singapore into a First World country by the time Lee Kuan Yew stepped down as prime minister in 1990 (although he would remain in the Cabinet as a mentor). This was a truly remarkable achievement. Things went well until the Asian Crisis of 1997 devastated the economies of South East Asia. Although Singapore was not itself in crisis, it was impacted as the main financial centre for the region. This was followed by a series of shocks—the bursting of the information technology bubble in 2000, the 9/11 attacks in New York and the panic over the SARS epidemic in 2002. All of these events hurt Singapore.

The government then decided to take a gamble and turn Singapore into Asia's 'Global City'. It was an audacious idea. Other global cities like London and New York had evolved organically over a very long time, but Singapore would attempt to deliberately turn into one by strategically encouraging sectors like higher education, entertainment and international finance. Within a decade, the skyline was transformed by iconic towers and 'supertrees' while the influx of professionals for the new sectors pushed the population to 5.5 million (more than double the 1.9 million at independence). When Lee Kuan Yew passed away in 2015, he left behind a city that was arguably the most advanced in the world.

A New Dawn in South Africa

The years 1990 and 1991 witnessed major shifts in world history. The Soviet Union, till then considered a superpower, collapsed without a shot being fired. The Indian Ocean rim too saw major changes. After decades of following a socialist economic model, India finally began to liberalize its economy. This would have profound implications for India's economic and social trajectory. In South Africa, the apartheid regime finally began to crumble. Nelson Mandela was released from prison in February 1990 after twenty-eight years. He had kept the faith for all those years and on three occasions had rejected conditional offers of release. After his release, he took over as the leader of the African National Congress and began the difficult process of negotiations that would finally end white minority rule.

To the outside world, South Africa's internal tensions appeared as black-versus-white, but the situation on the ground was much more complicated. The white population was split between those who favoured the changes and those who clung on to hopes of some form of return to segregation. There were also the old suspicions between English-speaking whites of British origin and Afrikaans-speaking Boers of Dutch origin. The wounds of the Boer wars of 1880–1881 and 1899–1902 had still not been completely healed. The black population was similarly divided on tribal lines. The Zulu nationalist Inkatha Freedom Party was suspicious of the African National Congress (Nelson Mandela and many ANC leaders are from the rival Xhosa tribe). As the apartheid regime crumbled, these rivalries increasingly spiralled into bloodshed. In just one of the incidents, dubbed the Boipatong massacre, forty people were killed and many more were injured. By the summer of 1993, all sides were stockpiling arms.

As if this was not complicated enough, there were still other groups including Indians and those of mixed race. The latter formed a large segment of the population in the western half of the country, but found themselves stuck in a cultural and political no man's land. The Indian population was scattered but formed a significant concentration around the eastern city of Durban. Although it had faced discrimination under apartheid, the industrious community had come to control much of the country's retail and wholesale trade and had become fairly prosperous. Not surprisingly, all other groups resented them. In fact, virtually every group suspected that the Indians were funding its rivals!

The South Africa we see today owes much to the philosophical evolution and personal example of one man. It would have taken very little for the country to have gone into a spiral of violence and retribution and turned out as another Zimbabwe or even another Somalia. It is Nelson Mandela's extraordinary achievement that he was able to somehow reconcile the country's many internal contradictions and carry people along with him. Equally commendable is the fact that, unlike many leaders of newly freed countries, he did not yield to the temptation of holding on to power till his death or starting a dynasty. He became president in 1994 and stepped down in 1999 after just one term. Modern historians tend to be dismissive of the 'Great Man Theory' of history, but Mandela and Lee Kuan Yew are proof that individuals do matter. It is noteworthy that, despite being very determined leaders, both of them allowed their philosophies and ideas to evolve with changing circumstances. Therein may lie the secret of their success.

The Evolution of Mumbai

The evolution of Mumbai encapsulates the social and economic changes witnessed by India since independence. When India became a Republic in 1950, Calcutta was no longer the capital but it was still the most important commercial and cultural centre. With a population of 2.6 million, it was by far the largest urban cluster in the country. Bombay was India's second largest city with a population of almost 1.5 million. Bombay's financial and commercial heart was still in and around the old Fort area, although an extension had been added in the form of Ballard Estate during the First World War. Further north, the cotton mills of Lower Parel hummed with activity and attracted migrants. Although modern innovations like telephones and automobiles were leading to changes in how business was done, this was still a world that would have been recognizable to Premchand Roychand.

The first big shift came in the 1970s with the construction of Nariman Point on reclaimed land near the southern tip of the island (not far from Fort), which created a cluster of relatively modern (although rather ugly) corporate offices. The city's success in attracting corporate offices was helped by the decline of Calcutta, which was wracked by violence from Naxalites and militant trade unionism in the 1970s and 1980s. As the old capital declined, companies shifted their headquarters to Bombay. This city too witnessed a period of labour unrest, which led to the closure of many mills in the Lower Parel area, but Bombay's overall business culture remained intact and it emerged as India's commercial capital. In 1990–91, India's socialist economic model collapsed and the crisis forced the country to start liberalizing the economy. The corrupt system of industrial licensing was dismantled and rules were eased for foreign investment. As foreign banks and multinationals entered the country, they bid up prices of the limited stock of commercial real estate and, within a few years, Nariman Point, in Bombay, had some of the most expensive real estate in the world. The country's business elite was a small club and everyone who mattered lived and worked in the southern tip of Bombay in the 1990s.

Given the spiralling real estate prices, a poor migrant had little choice other than to live in a slum, but even a white-collar newcomer, with a well-paying job, would have to either rent a room as a 'paying guest' or opt for a far-off northern suburb like Borivali or Kandivali. Since jobs were concentrated in the southern tip, the office day began with a long journey in a tightly packed train followed by a hop by 'share taxi' to one's office; in the evening, one did the same thing in reverse. This rough commute still defines the experience of many.

By the turn of the century, however, the dynamics of the city began to change. The old, derelict mills of Lower Parel were gradually converted into offices, condominiums and malls. Further north, a new financial district emerged in Bandra-Kurla. This created new hubs of activity in the middle of the city. Office towers and five-star hotels mushroomed even further north near the international airport. Within a decade, most banks and corporates shifted from Nariman Point to the glass-and-chrome towers of these new clusters. In many ways, these changes democratized the city as the old elite gave way to a confident new middle class. Thus, Bombay became Mumbai.

The Churn of History

The long history of the Indian Ocean is one where the unfolding of events is the result of complex interactions between myriad factors—the monsoon winds, geography, human migrations, technology, religion, culture, the deeds of individuals and, perhaps, occasionally the whims of the gods. It followed no predetermined path or grand plan, but is the story of long cycles, dead ends and unintended consequences, of human triumphs and extraordinary bravery but also of treachery and inexplicable human cruelty. There are many shades of grey along the way.

The complex, adaptive nature of history is a warning that a linear narrative based on a unidimensional framework is necessarily misleading. A corollary is that the path of history flows neither from nor to Utopia. Indeed, the attempts to 'civilize' others and impose utopias have been the source of much human misery and are almost always based on some unidimensional interpretation of history. This book has been written at a time when the Indian Ocean rim is enjoying a period of peace and prosperity after many centuries of colonization, war and famine. However, the failed state of Somalia and renewed hostilities in Yemen remind us how fragile this peace can be.

It is also remarkable how many continuities have remained through all these centuries of change. The monsoon winds may no longer dictate where ships can sail, but they are still important to the economic lives of hundreds of millions who depend on them for the annual rains. Some continuities run so deep that we hardly notice them. For instance, certain ancient cultural ideas continue to impact us to this day despite layers of later influences. We saw how matrilineal customs were an important aspect of history in the eastern but not in the western Indian Ocean rim. Perhaps this explains why we have seen so many female leaders in Eastern Indian Ocean countries, including Corazon Aquino, Megawati Sukarnoputri,

Aung San Suu Kyi, Indira Gandhi, Sheikh Hasina, Sirimavo Bandaranaike to name just a few. While researching this book, I also came across numerous instances of how the lives of ordinary individuals had been impacted by the churn of people and empires in the Indian Ocean.

Take, for instance, the story of Odakkal Mohammad who was born on 15 August 1927 in Mundappalam (now in the state of Kerala). His family claimed descent from Yemeni merchants who had settled here in the fourteenth century. In 1942, when barely fifteen, he was thrown out of school for wearing a black badge in protest against the arrest of Mahatma Gandhi. Too scared of being scolded by his father for this, Mohammad decided to run away from home and eventually ended up in the Royal Indian Navy as an electrical artificer. The Second World War was raging at that time and Mohammad saw action on a number of occasions. After the war, he was posted to Bombay where he would participate in the Naval Revolt of 1946. When the mutiny was suppressed, he was dismissed from the navy with a certificate that read: 'Discharged in Disgrace from His Majesty's Service'. Mohammad tore up the paper and flung it at the British officer. The following year, India became independent on his twentieth birthday.

Since the mutineers were never reabsorbed into the navy, Mohammad tried his hand at many jobs before getting involved in protests against Portuguese rule in Goa in 1955. He was arrested by the Portuguese and spent some time in prison before being released. After several more adventures, including cycling across India, he became a tour guide in Agra where he met and married a Christian nurse Mariamma on 15 August 1964. Decades later, he would return to his village in Kerala where he was living at the time this book was written. This extraordinary story was narrated to me by his son Commodore Odakkal Johnson as we hunted, amidst torrential monsoon rain, for an almost forgotten memorial for WWI sailors in Mumbai's old port area.

This book is concerned with the past, but the wheels of history roll relentlessly forward. What does the future hold? Even as I was completing this book, there were signs that the Indian Ocean may become the theatre of a new geopolitical rivalry between India and China. Those who remember history will know that the Indian Ocean has seen the likes of Rajendra Chola and Zheng He before. They will also know to expect the unexpected. After all, no one who saw Zheng He's magnificent Treasure Fleet would have believed that, a few decades later, a small country in the Iberian peninsula would open the Indian Ocean to centuries of European domination. If there is one lesson from this history, it is this: Time devours the greatest of men and the mightiest of empires.